From the
Bering Strait

and other stories

Winners of the 1999 Fish Publishing Short Story Prize

Introduction by Molly McCloskey

Edited by Clem Cairns

Assistant Editors
Jula Walton
Yann Kelly-Hoffman
Jennifer Corcoran

Fish Publishing
Durrus, Bantry, Co. Cork
Ireland

Published in Ireland by
Fish Publishing, 1999
Durrus, Bantry, Co. Cork

This book is published with the assistance of both Arts Councils in Ireland.

The Arts Council
An Chomhairle Ealaíon

**ARTS
COUNCIL**
of Northern Ireland

ISBN 0 9523522 7 3
A catalogue record of this book is available from the British Library.

Cover Painting, *Afternoon Swimmer,* by Gabrielle Seymour.

For further details on Fish Publishing's annual short story prize see the back of this book, or
write to:

Fish Publishing Short Story Prize
Durrus
Bantry
Co. Cork
Ireland

Or see our web site - www.sleeping-giant.ie/fishpublishing

This book is for
Roddy Doyle

Contents

Editor's Note

This is the fifth anthology from the Fish Short Story Prize. The competition is established. No longer do we receive stories about 'how I caught my first trout'. People know. Arts councils all over the world inform writers. Libraries, writers-in-residence, county and city arts officers, writing group leaders, writers' magazines all spread the word. Thanks to all of you.

Gina Ochsner, from Oregon, was the overall £1,000 winner with her story *From The Bering Strait,* from which the book takes its title. Congratulations to her for a wonderful story in a field of high quality.

The aim of the competition is to discover new and exciting talent, while not making any sacrifice to quality. This anthology is a tribute to the writers who entered. Thank you for your originality, your effort, courage, sweat and tears. While there is only room for eighteen stories, we received many more that could have made it. I encourage you all to keep writing. Your stories and your insights are valuable. It does not go unnoticed that you ache and toil, agonize type and spend unhealthy amounts of hours in solitude!

Frank McCourt, Molly McCloskey, and Alex Keegan were the final arbiters. It was big–spirited and generous of these busy people to lend their time and expertise. Thank you!

Shortlisting were Yann and Clare Kelly-Hoffman, Frank O'Donovan, Jennifer Corcoran, Francis Humphries, and Jamie McCarthy-Fisher. This was a difficult task and often the cause of sleepless nights. They did a terrific job.

Three of the winners this time have featured before, Martin Malone, Geraldine Taylor, and Ian Wild. They are thereby disqualified from entering again, barred by their excellence. All are working on longer projects and are not far off publication. Look out for their books.

For the next competition two more prizes have been added to the £1,000 first prize, a week at the Anam Cara Writers' and Artists' Retreat in West Cork, and a weekend of creative writing at Dingle Writing Courses Ltd, Co. Kerry. We realize that not everyone will be able to avail of these, as winners come from all over the world. In such cases the prizes will be transferred to the next person. Details of these prizes are at the back of this book. We are hoping to add to the prizes over the coming months. We are also providing a critiquing service for writers who are looking for feedback. There will be a fee for this. For updates on this and other competition information write to us or see our website — www.sleeping-giant.ie/fishpublishing

The judges for the first Short Story Prize of the new millennium are William Wharton, author of many books including *Birdy, Dad, A Midnight Clear;* Julia Darling, author of *Crocodile Soup;* and Dermot Bolger, author of *The Woman's Daughter, Finbar's Hotel,* and several other novels and plays. The closing date is 30th November.

The painting featured on the cover of this book is called *Afternoon Swimmer* by Gabrielle Seymour. It was the winner of the £500 Fish Art Prize. Thanks to all who entered, judge Pat Connor had a very difficult time selecting from your work. The standard was exceptional. The closing date for next year is 14th February, 2000. You can write to us for details or see our website.

To all of you writers and artists, good luck. To the readers of this book, I hope you enjoy it.

Clem Cairns, Durrus, 1999

Introduction

In Frank O'Connor's short story, *News for the Church*, Father Cassidy (known for his leniency) advises a young woman in his confessional: 'It's all the little temptations we don't indulge in that give us true refinement.' What a perfectly ambiguous piece of moral instruction. What music to our ears. What more could we ask for in the way of loopholes? For who is to say which are the little and which the not-so-little? How do you separate them? (Deliberation, reflection, a bit of time, but then not one of those keeps much company with temptation.) You could find yourself fudging, engaging in all sorts of intellectual gymnastics in order to allow yourself to call small *big*. On the other hand, if you really felt the need to go to such lengths, maybe that particular temptation wasn't so little after all. Otherwise, why would you have bothered?

But wait a minute. Is it really the venials we need avoid? We thought those were the freebies, the forgivables, the ways of letting off steam, to keep us out of really big trouble. But then we're talking about refinement here, not salvation. And what *about* refinement? It too seems a pretty relative term. What I call refined, you call retentive, or vice versa. Too much refinement and you tighten into preciousness, prudishness. You seize up. You're no fun anymore. You can put people off with too much refinement, and that'll pretty much take care of temptation for you.

So yes, as ethics, that piece of advice has its problems. But as aesthetics, and as a comment on the art of the short story itself, it seems perfectly apt. Because in the story, there's only so much space, and you can't have everything. Nor can you give it. Knowing what to hold back, what not to do, or say, is such a part of a story's shaping. So that the story itself becomes a kind of enticement. Like being led by the hand to a particularly fascinating keyhole. But a keyhole, nonetheless. And right there, along with whatever slice of life we've glimpsed, are all the things we don't know, or aren't told, or haven't fully understood. And that's the beauty of it. That knowing everything would only spoil the view.

From the Bering Strait, by Gina Ochsner, is this year's winning story. With its strange mixture of pained resignation, intimate involvement, and almost detached curiosity, it reads a little like a *Letter from* . . . , one of those daily missives we find in our newspapers, a communiqué penned from some exotic location in which unthinkable, often catastrophic, things are taking place. In this case, from where the ice caps have expanded, and the annual thaw, finally, has just stopped coming. There used to be 'springs of wet snow and starlings, springs of impossible, violent blue skies'. But now, words and tears turn quickly to ice and, out of self-preservation, the inhabitants have 'by unspoken consensus decided to try not to talk or sweat or bleed or cry . . . exposing any of our bodily fluids is a very dangerous thing to do. Still, we make mistakes.'

This story steps so lightly. Nothing is made overly much of, as though that kind of defeatism has set in where tragedies have come to seem commonplace. 'There's a funeral every other day, it seems, but nobody cries, of course.' But despite its understatement, or perhaps because of it, it's a beautifully powerful story.

To say that the story is a metaphor for some other kind of icing over – the days when, alone, we recall a past full of violent blue skies – is to suggest a certain contrivance which doesn't exist. It's just that the story is steeped in loss, in a way that is suggestive of more than its literal self. Children freeze to death, a friend dies drinking antifreeze and is found in a puddle of liquid (' . . . the striations of neon green and cobalt blue. If a peacock feather melted, maybe it would look like this . . . '), but then there's this business about the roses, as though if only the narrator and his wife can coax them forth through one more spring, the freeze will not have won.

But the roses don't come, and his wife is succumbing to the

lethal cold:

'I think about what Dolores might be feeling, how it feels to slowly freeze, about how I am feeling. I think about how your heart still beats like it always did, but there is a tightness . . . Your heart is fighting to break free from the weight of the cold. And then your heart, over time, doesn't fight as hard as it did the day before. And so it goes, and so it goes, until one day your heart just stops.'

Despite the story's title, there is a timelessness and a placelessness to it that raises it out of itself. It's wonderful.

In *This is Art*, a story by Maureen Aitken, the jauntiness, the gently flippancy, fail to mask the underlying melancholy. Nor are they meant to. The thirty-something narrator suffers from that premature weariness that comes from living in an overly ironic time. She works at an art institute, her boyfriend in a computer graphics firm – 'creating mountains' or putting cars on the moon. ('They want them on the moon now. The earth isn't good enough anymore.') In this world of created surfaces – where fast-food joints stretch in the distance 'like telephone poles, or stop signs', repeating and repeating 'until the eye could not know to see them anymore' – she is trying hard to trust in something. In sincerity, or love, or maybe in trust itself. A mildly subversive act, in her world. This is a deceptively quiet story, punctuated by small epiphanies, moments of marvellous illumination.

Geraldine Taylor's story, *Etienne's Tattoo*, is a strange – and strangely compelling – tale which isn't nearly as whimsical as its title suggests. It's about two women friends, but it reads more like a love story, the narrator utterly besotted by Etienne, this 'grotesque, repulsive and utterly beautiful' woman. They meet in a motorway service station when Etienne says, 'When men stare like *you're* staring they're wondering how it *is* with me . . . What's your excuse, my friend?'

Dialogue carries a lot of weight in short stories. In good ones, it's almost as though the characters know they've got ten seconds here and another ten there and if they choose their lines wisely, they can tell us everything that's worth knowing about them.

Etienne is peppered with just such dialogue. And the effect is that uncanny experience we can have when reading, of coming to know one character through the eyes of another – through the eyes of a narrator who's never quite understood, but makes certain that we do.

In *A Face in the Wallpaper*, by Hugo Kelly, so much happens just off stage. Something's wrong at home, something's wrong with Mr Canning, too, who owns the local pub. The boy at the centre of the story seems a little disturbed; he sees faces in the wallpaper, a stuffed fox talks to him. The boy narrates in the second person: 'The delta of meeting rivers on the cracked ceiling hold your attention. If you close your eyes you can hear their Amazonian roar. The diamonds that live in the carpet dance around you if you stare without blinking for long enough. The stairs to the attic is dark and there is a smell of old clothes and of another age that seems less bright than your own.'

The child's perspective immerses us in a mental world where very little that's seen is really understood. And when, in this case, whatever is seen is so disturbing, the second-person narration reminds us of how we can set about creating for ourselves an artificial distance from events, in order to survive them. As though it really were possible to be at one remove, to experience a story we're in the midst of as though it were happening to someone else.

There's humour in this collection too. *Heard of a Band Called Mysterical?*, by Mick Wood, is a very funny send-up of the rock'n'roll fantasy of an ill-fated garage band in its infancy. The narration reads like a deadpan, cinematic voice-over, which is utterly appropriate, as one of the band member's favourite activities is imagining the documentaries that will one day be made about them. 'Some years later (but not *too* many) as a moment in an MTV retrospective, and by way of poignant contrast, the ascent of these grotty steps is cut with shots of them mounting the stage in a vast stadium.'

The narrator shows little mercy, recounting every risible act, each self-conscious attempt at *star quality*, but somehow never losing his affection for his characters. There are wonderful walk-ons by con men and music industry has-beens. There is behind-the-scenes intrigue: before Mysterical has even played its first gig, egos are clashing, interlopers are muscling in. A teenage girl wanting to edge out the female lead singer, advises an infatuated band member: 'All bands have their casualties. It'll be in the first chapter of the autobiography, how you had to make the difficult but essential decision to lose that girl.' She seems perfect for the band: no talent, but with an eye on posterity.

Pam Leeson's story – *the forces* – is a story *about* the unsaid. It's a record of missed opportunities and miscommunication, the pathos of signals utterly misread. What we actually read is a long dialogue consisting of everything two people (a couple on an outing) do *not* say to each other. When they do occasionally speak, it's only to say the very opposite of what they're thinking. The lack of capitalisation, the lack of punctuation, the very layout of the story, combine to heighten the sense that we are listening to two interior monologues impossibly in conversation with one another. The mild departures from logical progression or literal coherence, the quick ping-ponging of thoughts, produce in the reader a funny sense of vertigo, a dizzying disorientation that's wholly appropriate to the subject matter. But the story has its own sense of order and as it progresses, swells towards a cumulative truth.

Every story in this book makes its own original way in the world. Knowing which are the telling moments, and showing them to us. Holding back when necessary. And as the narrator of the winning story casually remarks, 'Sometimes, it's the small things that really amaze me.'

Molly McCloskey, Sligo, 1999

Gina Ochsner

Overall Winner of the 1999 Fish Short Story Prize

Just for the record, I have never actually lived in Alaska, though I have always heard that it is bitterly cold up there. My uncle and aunt lived there for several years, and will swear on a stack of Bibles that if you step outside to relieve yourself during a deep freeze, you can actually create a frozen yellow arc in the air. I don't know if that's really gospel truth, but that story and my incredible fear of freezing gave rise to *Bering Strait*. Now I am trying to keep up with our three-year-old son, Connor, and our two snow dogs: a Siberian Husky and a Malamute who I hope will someday pull us to an Iditorod win.

From the Bering Strait

Gina Ochsner

Up here at the top of the country, the half-light gets trapped between double-paned windows. The light freezes and sticks there between the glass like a cold sap. The birds have a hard time getting around. Sometimes the ice catches them in mid-flight and for days they are stuck crooked in the freezing sky. If they are lucky, a warmer rain will unfix them, and if they are luckier still, none of their bones will snap from the shock of sudden flight, and they will fly south where they belong.

It wasn't always like this. We used to have springs of wet snow and starlings, springs of impossible, violent blue skies. But slowly it became clear as each year passed that winter was stealing days from spring, until eventually, the thaw stopped coming altogether. Those were the years the fish froze solid in the water and our children stopped growing.

I remember the last true spring. The thaw came in the middle of the night, *like the bridegroom for the bride*, my wife, Dolores, says to anyone who wants to hear the story of the Last Thaw. There we were lying in our bed. The sun had set early, so the sky was black and thick as liver. We heard a groaning like some huge animal was sleeping below the ice and beginning to wake, to claw its way out. Then we heard a terrific crack, like the sound of a bone snapping, only much louder. We lay still in our bed, afraid to breathe because when the break-up happens, for a moment you're not sure if it's the thaw or an earthquake. Then I leapt out of bed, ran to the kitchen, and brought back a bottle of wine and two glasses.

"American Beauty," Dolores said, touching her glass to mine.

"Royal Princess," I said.

This was the game we played, naming prize-winning roses from the rose catalogues. This was how we welcomed spring, planning our gardens, worrying over the beds, mulch, the enriched soil fortified by worm castings.

When we walk outside, even the hairs in our nostrils freeze stiff and it hurts to breathe. And here's another problem: our words and tears turn to ice on the tips of our tongues or in the corners of our eyes. It's hard to tell them apart, too, because when they chip off and fall, they look like little slivers of glass caught on our moustaches, sleeves, and the tips of our shoes. To cope with these problems, we have by unspoken consensus decided to try not to talk or sweat or bleed or cry. We have come to discover that exposing any of our bodily fluids is a very dangerous thing to do. Still, we make mistakes.

Last week, Mushie broke into the pharmacy and helped himself to a packet of codeine tablets and a few ccs of morphine. Then just yesterday he did himself in on antifreeze. It had to have hurt like hell, like swallowing a Cuisinart jammed on high, but maybe, for a minute or two, he felt warm. They say that's what happens when you die, just as you are dying, even as you are freezing to death, for one euphoric second, you are on fire.

I knew something was wrong when I saw his dogs tangled up in front of the pharmacy. They were baying and howling, trying to push through the front door of the pharmacy, but Mushie had left them hooked up to the sled and the sled was jammed up in the frame of the door. I unharnessed them and they tripped over each

2

other, trying to get to Mushie.

In the puddle of liquid that surrounded him I could see the striations of neon green and cobalt blue. If a peacock feather melted, maybe it would look like this. I smelled the plastic gallon jug of antifreeze. It was oily and a little sweet. He had curled himself into foetal position so I rolled him to his knees, put my hands under his armpits, and dragged him outside to the sled. In this weather, he could have drank Freon and died quicker. This is not at all how I'd do it. And yet, I couldn't deny that with the way the colors seemed to melt around him, he was transformed somehow and that this was beautiful. I strapped him onto the sled. I rubbed off a few drips of antifreeze from around his mouth and pushed his eyelids closed with my thumb. I didn't bother harnessing the dogs. They followed the sled for about a mile and then veered off towards their kennels.

When I reached home, I wrote down on one of Dolores' yellow Post-it pads what I saw when I found Mushie. The puddle, the way he was hugging his knees, the way pearly drops of those brilliant colors of the Caribbean, that's what I actually wrote, colors of the Caribbean, pooled out around him like an oil slick. I wrote all this down because I thought it was important to remember, and because, of course, it would be too hard to say.

That night I carved a sculpture for him. I carved him with the flaps of his hat fastened down over his ears, his eyes squinting against the glare of the snow and laced tight against an invisible wind. That is the hard part – capturing motion, suggesting something that's not really there. I used a penknife for the lines in his face and around his eyes. If you keep a small pan of lukewarm water nearby, all you have to do is dip the knife once, lightly tap it against the side of the pan, and then the knife is warm and wet enough to make fluid cuts in the ice.

I worked on Mushie all night and through the next day. His hands were the hardest for me to sculpt. I wanted to show him as he was – one hand gripping reins and another holding a bottle or the whip, but for some reason, I couldn't get the fingers right. In the end, I hid his hands in the ruff of his dogs' fur. He is leaning forward on the sled, one elbow resting on the headboard, his other hand cradling his favorite dog, the lead, Skete.

I kept the garage door open so the wind could blow in flakes of snow. I sprinkled the dogs' coats with water because I wanted the snow to attach to the guard hairs so their fur would look fuzzy. It had taken me all day to shave long narrow slivers. Getting the fishhook curl into the ends of the shavings was the hardest part. I used one of Dolores' sewing needles as sort of a curling rod and exhaled slowly so that the ice would warm up slightly, curl, then refreeze. I was done and I let the wind score the ice a bit to give it the weathered look. Dolores came out, that yellow Post-it stuck to her index finger. She hadn't bothered to put her parka on, just her ratty old sweater. She looked at me for a long time. She folded her arms across her chest, bit her lip, and shivered.

"You're jealous. You're jealous he's dead," she said. Her words fell onto the concrete and shattered into jagged pieces.

"What?" I asked, covering my mouth with my hand. "Could you repeat that?" But of course she couldn't. She snapped off the garage lights and stepped into the house. I turned the light back on and kicked the pieces into the old snowdrift outside the garage.

People seem to think this cold must have happened overnight, that one day we just woke up and found ourselves in this mess. But when I look out all around me, I'm nearly blinded by the unending grey light and I know, it's coming, it's come, as regular and steady as my breathing. The blank sweep of the ice stretches on, everywhere, ice.

Dolores and I stay up late and we watch the television weather reports. One night they showed a segment about some gardener in Anchorage who coaxed some dwarf roses into bloom. Outside, the ice fell from the sky like old salt.

"The dirty bastard," Dolores said. I wheeled the TV out of the bedroom that very night. So now, I watch the TV by myself. The eerie, incandescent glow of the screen is the same strange shade of blue that the snow reflects under the Arctic light. People think snow is white, but if you look carefully in the shadows of the snow, you can see that it is really blue. When I go outside for a smoke, I think of those explosive blue skies of spring, Bering blue.

The weather bureau sent a team of researchers up here to study the freeze patterns. We all laughed as best as we could without freezing our lungs. You may have heard this kind of laugh before. It is a tortured sound, you wouldn't even think a human capable of it, but you'd be surprised. Anyway, they came in with their helicopter mounted with a special engine heater and all of their equipment – thermometers, barometers, dopplers, radars, and small satellite dishes. They even built a greenhouse. We couldn't figure out why. Up here, eaven in a greenhouse, it would be too cold for anything to grow. But they wanted to experiment and they insisted that certain northern hybrids of roses were suited for inclement weather. We all nearly lost it that time. The corners of my wife's eyes froze shut for two days. It was a laughless cry, though. And then she got sick and wouldn't get out of bed. One day, to cheer her up, I brought her pictures of roses.

"I almost forgot what they looked like," she said. She traced the edges of the roses with her finger. I taped pictures of roses all over the walls while she sat, propped up in bed, thumbing through the rose mail-order gardening catalogues like Burpies and Jackson and Perkin's and watching the gardening channel on cable TV.

"Fertilizer – that's very important," she muttered. I could barely hear her, she was so weak, and I knew what was happening to her – I could almost see it – the grey creeping past her ankles and up her shins. She tapped at a white JFK prize rose with her index finger. "You gotta feed those things – they're like people, you know."

5

My wife's mother calls almost every day. She wants to know what the hell is going on up here. I tell her that we are on the edge of a new ice age – a new millennium of freeze, that it is coming for her next, does she have enough light bulbs and toilet paper? The silence on her end of the phone is heavy and then she asks me if I'm still going to AA. I tell her that I quit because it was getting too crowded. She calls because she wanted to talk to Dolores, but talking is dangerous and Dolores is too sick to move.

More than once I'd thought of packing up and leaving. I was out the other day fuelling up my Dodge. But before I could even get the gas through the funnel, the gas had frozen solid. That's when I thought to myself that we could really be in trouble up here. And it's not that we don't have heaters or electric blankets, fireplaces and microwaves. In fact, one of the researchers has a tiny sun lamp. But it's like even with all these things, people can only take so much of this blistering cold. The thought that when you wake up that it is out there waiting for you is almost too much.

There's a funeral every other day, it seems, but nobody cries, of course. When our daughter died two months ago, I carved a swan family out of a huge ice block. The mother and father swan are nudging the swanlet into flight. The swanlet looks like it is flying right up out of that stump of ice, flying right out of this place.

"It's like the phoenix," Dolores said, dabbing at her eyes.

"Yesterday it was 80 in Phoenix – don't even *talk* to me about Phoenix," I said, running my fingers along the neck of the baby swan. She'll never melt away in this freeze, and I think that there's something perfect about all this cold.

Mushie found them, our daughter and her three high-school friends, on the way back from working out his team. The dogs started whining and pulling against their harnesses. They pulled Mushie towards what he thought were some dumb-shit optimistic ice-fishers. When the dogs saw them, they howled and tangled themselves up in their reins and refused to run. But the girls, they were sitting in a circle, holding hands, listening to Bob Marley. They were frozen stiff, bluer than blue, Mushie said, and the radio was still playing. Energizer batteries. Sometimes, it's the small things that really amaze me. I wrote to the CEO of the Energizer Batteries and told them how impressed I was with their batteries. I explained how my daughter's radio played forty-eight hours straight, no problem, in the middle of an Arctic freeze when everything else froze solid. The president wrote me back on Energizer stationery with that drum-pounding pink rabbit on the top, thanking me for my interest in the product. He wished there were more customers like me.

The weather bureau researchers are packing up and getting ready to leave. They're tired of the cold and they're afraid of what it could do to them. Someone threw an ice rock and shattered a square of the greenhouse and they've interpreted this action as a sign. They're leaving on the Swedish freightliner tomorrow even though they didn't finish collecting all the data. They're leaving in a flurry of equipment and printouts and the knowledge that maybe they've failed here. Still, it wasn't hard to get them to talk, once I gave them a bottle of gin and some long straws.

Two of the researchers thought that the ice caps had expanded and where we all thought we were living on frozen steppe, or permafrost, was actually an ice shelf, like an extension of Greenland. They explained that the cold was not only working above the ground, but below it as well, pushing the soil south and replacing it with ice, as far down as you'd care to dig, everywhere ice. There were some other theories: the polar disparity theory, the alien conspiracy theory. But my personal favorite came from the guy who brought the roses in. He attributed the cold to mass-hysteria. That's right – we're all hallucinating the freeze.

"Well, then, aren't we all a bunch of crazy fuckers," I said. He laughed, a choked sort of laugh and he forgot to cover his mouth with his scarf or mitten. Later, they had to load him on the freighter with a very real oxygen mask strapped to his face.

I check in on her every hour. Sometimes I read to her. I lean over and put my ear to her mouth to feel her breath because she's so still and turning such a strange shade of grey, I'm not sure she's alive. But today she caught me by surprise. I leaned over and she grabbed my arm, clenched it tight and pulled me down to her.

"Are the roses in bloom yet?" she asked. I wanted to buy her a whole garden of roses. I wanted to throw ice blocks at the green-house. I wanted to rip up those roses in there, grind the stalks up in my mouth, chew them up and spit them out.

"Well, are they?" she asked again. I looked at her lying there, at her purple lips and the tiny pearls of snot frozen on the end of her nose. I looked at her, held up by her pillows, and I lied to her.

"There's a very small, small but sturdy bud on the Jacob's Ladder."

"That's a climbing rose, a trailer."

"Yeah. Maybe a couple of weeks, it'll open, three weeks tops."

Sometimes I hate myself, I really do. She looked at me for a long time. She shouldn't do that – her eyes could freeze – and I was just about to remind her when she shut them at last. She collapsed against her pillows and the entire bed shuddered.

"I'm cold," she said. I put two more blankets on her, turned up the thermostat, and then I went outside.

I think about what Dolores might be feeling, how it feels to slowly freeze, about how I am feeling. I think about how your heart still beats as it always did, but there is a tightness as if papier mâché or plaster of Paris has been slathered over your heart and has now solidified. Your heart is fighting like a bird from within the shell, fighting to break free from the weight of the cold. And then your heart, over time, doesn't fight as hard as it did the day before. And so it goes, and so it goes, until one day your heart just stops. Literally stops cold. Like that. And it's true what they say, it's true

8

that when the cold consumes you, it consumes you completely, takes you as if it had been waiting for you your whole life. And when it does, all you can do is feel the weight of it crushing your chest, and you close your eyes then, and allow yourself this once to dream of the sun.

Eithne Le Goff

Winner of the 1999 Fish Short Story Prize

was born in 1960 and educated at UCD. She lives and works in Dublin. *A Game of Chess* is the first of her stories to be published, although another, *Childlights* will be published in the 1999 *Phoenix Irish Short Stories* anthology. The characters in *A Game of Chess* took on a life of their own and insisted on becoming part of a novel, *Stones in the River*, a gentle family tale of adultery, abuse, suicide, murder and madness.

A Game of Chess

Eithne Le Goff

The constant rain had prevented any of the children from taking their afternoon walk, and as a result, all of them were packed into the nursery, their numbers augmented by Edie, who had been forbidden from practising her scales on the drawing room piano by her stepmother. Everyone was in wicked spirits: Edie, dark and angry, was thumping with unnecessary force on the keys of the piano, Miss Balderein was even more inclined to weep than usual, Betsey was complaining that the wet weather brought on her arthritis and the twins were behaving as if collectively possessed by a hundred demons. Only baby Felicia was quiet, a situation unlikely to continue for long. The day nursery was hot and stuffy and Constance took refuge in the window seat, behind the red curtains which shielded her from the rest of the room. The barred windows had become steamed up from the heat inside, but Constance wiped a small patch clear and leaned her forehead against the cool glass. She could see a faint reflection of her face, thin and pale. Peering through, she searched for the heron who usually haunted the weir by the boathouse, but he too had taken refuge from the rain. All she could see was rain-sodden lawns and the brown river, and beyond that the dark mass of winter trees. Constance settled back in her seat. She was happy: she had her book with its pictures of Sherwood Forest, and she was trying her best to imagine herself there, in some cool green forest glade, with sympathetic companions and a life of freedom. The voices from outside kept interrupting, however: Miss Balderein was trying to teach the twins to read, a monumentally thankless task. Since Miss Balderein's duties had been augmented by the task of teaching the twins, Constance had been allowed a great deal more time to herself, a situation which pleased her greatly. Edie, at seventeen, still officially partook of lessons in German and French conversation with the governess, but as she despised Miss Balderein's Belgian accent she rarely paid any attention to them. She had learned French from the previous governess, a Parisian called Mademoiselle Jullien, whose disappearance from the household had caused her heart to break, as she had reminded the family on more than one occasion. She had had some slighting things to say about her father's judgement in employing Miss Balderein, but for once her stepmother, so often her ally in such vital matters as the necessity of obtaining a new bonnet or a sealskin winter coat, had sided with Mr Edgewood. Miss Balderein, mouse-like and pale, was as unlike the fiery and flirtatious Mademoiselle Jullien as was possible. And it was true, as Mr Edgewood claimed, that a governess who could claim both French and German as native tongues could be considered something of a bargain, even if her English, after nearly two years with the family, was still broken and unsure. Edie had often laughed at the fact that Miss Balderein was still struggling through *Jane Eyre*, the book she had begun just after her arrival from Brussels. Perhaps, Edie had mocked, she expected to follow in Jane's (and indeed their Stepmama's) footsteps and marry her employer: and the governess always blushed when Mr Edgewood made one of his rare visits to the nursery.

"You vicked children, vat haf you done to the pauvre chat?"

Miss Balderein sounded almost hysterical. Robert and Richard had succeeded in trapping Dinah the kitten and between them were attempting to see how far her seemingly elastic body could stretch. With an outraged yowl, however, the cat dug her claws into one set of hands and her teeth into another, and bounded for freedom to the top of the nursery cupboard, where she started to clean herself, apparently none the worse for her ordeal. Constance sighed. The day had started badly, with Betsey refusing to go down to the kitchen to fetch the twins more bread and milk for breakfast. As they had thrown most of their original breakfast over each other, Constance could hardly blame her: but unfortunately everyone in the nursery was being made to suffer the consequences of their hunger for the rest of the day.

The door clicked open: Constance started, then relaxed as she recognised the hesitant cough of Nan, who had come up with a bucket of coal to replenish the nursery fire. Nan said nothing: she rarely spoke unless spoken to and when she did her accent was so strong and her speech so uncertain it was as if she were trying to speak a foreign language. Betsey had told Constance that Nan had only been able to talk Irish when she first came to the household. That had been eleven years before, when Constance was a baby. Nan had been found destitute, a small child left alone in the street near the park gate. Perhaps, like so many other refugees from the west, she had been on her way to Liverpool with her parents. It seemed most likely that her parents had died, along with countless others: in any event they had disappeared without trace. The child could not even tell them her name, and even when she learned to speak English she never seemed to be able to give any coherent information on her past. Constance's mother had called her Nan West, had her baptised in the Protestant church and given her a place in the household.

The nursery door clicked again, but this time it was flung open and George entered the room.

There was a clatter as Nan dropped the coal shovel, Edie hit a dud note on the piano and Constance pulled herself a little further behind the curtains.

"Nan, be careful there, will you," said Betsey sharply, adding more quietly, "you can leave that now, like a good girl, and go on downstairs."

Constance peeped out and saw Nan bob towards Betsey and scuttle to the door, her eyes downcast and her face red.

With a large smile and an exaggerated bow, George held the door open for her as she made her way out.

"Master George, come in now and shut the door, don't be letting all the heat out. And don't slam it: you'll wake the baby. What brings you up here, in any case? Should you not be doing your lessons?"

"But I'm bored, Betsey: and it's too wet to go riding, or shooting, or fishing: it's even too wet to go up to the barracks to watch the manoeuvres. I'm thoroughly out of sorts, so I have come to see my beloved sisters – and my half-brothers too, of course."

Betsey sniffed. There was a silence in the room: even the twins seemed subdued by George's entrance, although he was always the first to encourage them in any mischief they might have planned. Today, however, he was very much the young master, striding over to where they were laboriously copying sentences onto their slates. Large, florid George was indeed beyond most people's control: even the control of the masters in his school in England, for he had been sent home early for the Christmas holidays, with instructions that his presence was no longer desirable. No one in the nursery knew exactly why he had been sent home, with the possible exception of Betsey, who knew everything but merely tightened her lips when she was asked.

Now he stood directly behind Miss Balderein as she guided Robert's hand to form letters on the slate. Taller than she, he leaned over to peer at the text.

"It is good to see the twins making progress," he said in an avuncular tone which he had carefully copied from his father. "But Miss B., is there not a grammatical error in the sentence they are copying?"

Panicked, Miss Balderein stared at the sentence she had so

scrupulously prepared.

"Perhaps – indeed – but indeed I should be more careful, indeed I try my best," she started to stutter, desperately trying to find her mistake. George smiled suddenly and said, "Ah, perhaps not. Perhaps it is correct after all."

He straightened and glanced around the room, then caught a glimpse of Constance peering cautiously from behind the curtain. He raised his eyebrows.

"What, sis, hiding in corners? Tch, indeed you should be more social. Come out and play a game of chess with your brother."

Constance hesitated. She could say that she was reading, and risk having the book snatched from her and being pulled from the window seat with much poking and prodding, or she could hope that George would lose interest in the game after a few moments and leave the nursery. Alternatively, the game could result in one of his rages, those terrible rages which seemed to blow up out of nowhere.

"Well, Connie, are you coming or do I have to get you?"

George was beginning to sound impatient. Constance came out of her haven and made her way to where George was standing in front of the fireplace, his coat-tails up, blocking the heat from everyone else in the room.

She took down the chess set and began to lay out the pieces, black against white on the board. They had played chess together for many years, but although George had often lost his temper when there seemed to be a faint possibility he might not win, it was only lately that Constance had tried to avoid playing with him altogether, when he had begun to insist on laying bets and dares and forfeits for the loser. It had begun last summer, at the time when she had started to find that her refuge in the boathouse was constantly occupied by George. The boathouse had been the place where she had felt safe and at peace with the world, the water lapping against the weathered wooden walls and the shadowy light like that of an underwater kingdom. George would

creep up behind her and insist on playing catch. The games were
starting to take on an edge of something she understood little and
liked even less. All she knew was that she did not want her brother
to catch her and that since George had come home she often
woke in the night with bad dreams, nightmares of being pursued
through endless corridors and threatening forests, with Edie,
irritable and sleepy, pinching her awake so that she would stop
muttering and twitching.

"So," said George, "the winner shall have their choice of
wager."

"What wager?" asked Constance cautiously.

"The winner shall decide!" George laughed triumphantly.
"Come along, sit down. I shall be white and you shall be black."

"So you move first."

Constance knew the rules of chess but was no match for
George, four years older and with a great deal more practice in
playing the game. She knew it was a hopeless battle: she could
only watch the progress of George's pieces moving relentlessly
over the board, taking piece after piece of her black army. She
drifted away from concentrating on the game to listen to Betsey,
who had relieved Miss Balderein of the twins and was telling them
stories as she turned sheets by the fire. Sometimes Betsey told
stories of the Good People: of stolen babies, of children taken
away for what seemed to them to be no more than a night but who
found, on their return, that their playmates were greybeards and
their parents long dead. Today she was telling a family story, a
tale she had often told to Constance, about her mother's last days
and the arrival of Nan.

"The first Mrs Edgewood – that was the mother of Edie and
Constance and George – she was never right after Constance was
born. She used to sit at the window at the front of the house and
watch the road. It was a black year – '48 – and the worst of the
great hunger. Thousands were starving or dying of fever in the
west. Those that could made their way eastwards, to the docks

16

where they would get a boat to Liverpool and from there a passage to America. They would be walking right past this house to get down to the quays."

George interrupted: "That's when our father changed his business from moving coal to moving people and made a great deal of money. He told me so. '48 was his windfall year. But he says he is not sure the trade will last – there are so many rules and regulations and investigations now. That's one of the reasons why he won't have us move to Rathmines."

Edie stopped her practice and said impatiently: "But it's ridiculous to live here – it is so unfashionable now, nothing but labourers and paupers. Papa just wants to stay here because of the fishing in the Liffey. But there is no society. Stepmama is right: we should move."

"Aye," said Betsey, somewhat acidly. "And then she will get away from all the folk that remember her mother's people from the Mill. I suppose she'd rather no one knew about them."

Edie sniffed. She felt a certain loyalty to her stepmother, who often asked her advice and confided in her the many difficulties of the lady of the house: controlling servants, managing the budget, obtaining white lilac at a reasonable price. Both of them found Betsey particularly difficult to keep in her place.

"Well," she said, "I do not think there is anything wrong with trying to better oneself, to move in polite circles. It is admirable – and after all, her father was a clergyman, and she was trained as a governess, which is quite a genteel occupation."

"I would never call the mistress anything other than genteel, Miss Edie," said Betsey, perhaps aware that she had overstepped her place. "We all know what a support she has been to the master in his grief."

George snorted. "Whatever his grief he did not wait very long after Mama had died to marry her. Our Mama," he continued, addressing the twins – "was a lady: a real one: she had a title, from her own family – they had a big estate in the country, near

Sligo."

"But she was mad," said Robert, looking puzzled. "That's what *our* Mama says."

There was a moment's shocked silence in the nursery and then Betsey said sharply: "Never say such a thing again, Master Robert. That is a terrible thing to be saying. The first mistress was no more mad than you or I – just sick and sad. She was never herself again after the birth of Miss Constance, though a quieter, bonnier wee baby you could never hope to look after. But she was always a kind and a good lady. She was the one who took in Nan. I was telling you how she used to watch the travellers on the road. This would be the last bit of their journey. Some came in wagons paid for by their landlords, but mostly they walked, and a more miserable set of starving, filthy creatures you never saw. They came in droves, as if the west wind was bringing them along with the rain. It was a terrible sight, and I often told my mistress that she would do no good to them or herself staring at them from her chair like a ghost. The strangest thing about them was the silence – they were like no other crowd I've ever seen, anywhere: no chat or songs or stories. Not a sound out of even the babies . . . Hundreds and hundreds of them had died along the sides of the roads, and what was left was like an army of ghosts. It was a bad time for everyone – except, of course, as you said, Master George, for those in the shipping business."

"But why were they starving?" asked Richard.

"Ach, the potatoes, that most of the poor creatures lived on, were after getting a disease – a blight – and failed. After that they had nothing to eat and the cholera and typhoid came, and it seems things just got worse and worse, like. Sure they are still leaving, you can still see gangs of them along the road, for none of them poor creatures out in the west has got over it yet."

"Thomas said it is because the English rule us and we should be free, and have our own government."

Constance rarely ventured an opinion, but she was hoping the turn the conversation had taken would keep George's attention off the game. If she could make it last until it was time for nursery tea perhaps the game would never be finished, and there would be no forfeit to pay. She was trying to mirror his moves exactly, so that although she took none of his pieces, he could take none of hers without laying himself open to a counterattack on her part.

George looked up from the board and said angrily, "That is treasonous talk – he could be whipped for less."

Constance, slightly aghast at her own daring, continued: "And you said you hated England when you were in school there. You said they laughed at your accent and called you Paddy."

"That is different – although I would not expect you to understand. We are British, Constance: we are loyal to the Crown. . . . we have fought for it in countries all over the world. What is Ireland without Britain but a rain-soaked bog full of starving peasants? As British we are part of a great Empire, leaders in the world, leaders of civilisation."

He picked up his queen.

"Look," he said. "What is the most powerful piece on the board? It is this one: Britain is the Crown."

Constance stared at the board and thought of Queen Victoria. She was too young to remember Her Majesty's trip to Dublin, but she had heard stories of her visit.

"And these are the other pieces – there is the Church" – here he picked up a bishop – "and the army – that's the knight – and the castle is Dublin Castle, of course."

George was pleased with himself. He replaced the pieces – did they go back exactly where they had been? – and moved swiftly to capture Constance's remaining knight. Constance was suddenly aware of his foot touching hers under the table and moved her leg away sharply: too sharply for the safety of the low table on which the board was placed. Table and board flew up into the air and the pieces were scattered. George leapt up, scarlet with rage and cursing.

19

"What the devil are you doing?"

The room erupted into chaos. Edie stood up to remonstrate with her brother for his language, Betsey gathered the twins to her, but dropped them as the baby woke and began to cry; Miss Balderein, who had been bending low over the linen she was mending in the corner, left her work and came forward, showing a face once again tear-stained from homesickness: and Constance, in a panic, ran to the door and out of it before George could sufficiently gather his wits to strike a blow or catch her.

She was sobbing for breath as she ran down the dark corridors, past the mahogany panelling and occasional tables decorated with their vases of white lilies, past coloured-glass windows that made the floors and walls look stained with blood, past the stairs to the attics, where the maids and the two daughters of the first family slept. Downstairs, past the parlour that was her stepmother's domain, past the library, her father's sanctuary where no child dared set foot without his permission. That left one place, which was seldom visited by anyone in the household: her mother's room, the Green Room where she had died. Constance never went in there, afraid of meeting the ghost of the woman she could only remember from the picture in the nursery. A pale lady, with dark hair, in a dress that seemed spun out of starshine. In earlier days, George had often teased her when she swore she could remember her mother bending over her to kiss her goodnight in that very dress. Now she prays to her mother to save her from whatever is coming behind her in the shape of George's angry form. Turning the bend, she glances behind her: George is not yet in sight. She pushes open the door to the Green Room and shuts it as quietly as she can behind her, leaning for a moment against the carved wood. The room is filled with a dim light, with a faint smell of must. Where to hide? Under the bed with its patriotically green hangings? Behind the window curtains? In the heavy mahogany wardrobe with its glass panels in the doors? Where is safety? She runs quickly to the wardrobe and pulls the door shut behind her as she crawls into a world of fur and feather, silk and velvet. Pushing past old ballgowns and animal skins, she squeezes herself into the back, sobbing in her throat:

"Please don't let him catch me, please don't let him catch me." And then comes the part that seems hardest to explain, even to herself in later life. She will always be unsure of exactly what happened, and whenever she tries to grasp it, the sequence of events slips away to the edge of her mind, beyond her reach. Perhaps it was a miracle, perhaps a gift of temporary madness from her dead mother. There are dreadful times later in her life when something like it happens again: but this is the first time.

As she pushes past her mother's clothes, further into the refuge of the wardrobe, the smell of mothballs making the breath catch in the back of her throat – more afraid than ever in her life before – for if George finds her here there will be no escape – the oddest thing happens. She is aware of the door opening, of George's footsteps in the room, of his voice saying, "Boh! Madam Mouse – I know you are in there."

Pushing her spine against the hard wood, Constance prays to her mother. She thinks hard of the stories she has read, the stories she has been told. She thinks of Sherwood Forest. She thinks of the girl in a Greek story, the one who sprouted green branches from her hands, who became part of the world of the wood. She is aware of her harsh breathing, of an overpowering smell of dust and mothballs. Thin shards of light filter through the gaps in the wood. Fur against her cheek, the touch of feathers against her nose, green silk around her feet and above her, a dress like starlight. She clenches her eyes shut, then her fists. The door of the wardrobe opens: she can hear George panting. He has her now. He stares for a moment, and Constance can hear both his breath and hers, unnaturally loud.

There is a long silence. Gradually, she becomes aware of light on her face, of faint rustlings and whisperings. Slowly she opens her eyes and finds herself in what seems to be a forest: green ferns grow where the silk dress has slid to the floor of the wardrobe, the wood behind her back is a living tree: a heron's bright glance looks down from a branch above her. Through her tears she can see stars shining through the network of branches above her head, a watery galaxy of light. She looks down but cannot see her hands, although she can feel them slowly unclenching in her lap. Like Robin Hood, like the Greek girl, like the Good People of Betsey's stories, like all those who have taken refuge in the forest, Constance has managed to make herself disappear.

Geraldine Taylor

Overall Second in the 1999 Fish Short Story Prize

Geraldine Taylor is a multi-award-winning writer of adult non-fiction, and children's fiction. She is Educational Consultant to Ladybird Books. Geraldine is also a University Student Counsellor.

Etienne's Tattoo

Geraldine Taylor

I'm going to open the box today: I'm going to look for answers.

Seeing as you ask, these are the things I want to know about Etienne:

1. Who was the lover who hurt her so badly?
2. What was the word she'd had tattooed at the top of her left thigh?
3. Where is she now?

Couple of years ago, there was a fourth thing: what was her real name? But that got answered when the police checked up with passport control. Her real name was (is?) Abigail Sutherland but she hadn't got the bulk for a name like that, she'd have been better off with a flimsy name the wind could whistle right through, like mine – Natalie. Anyway, Etienne suited her pretty good.

First time I saw Etienne, I sat across a table from her in a motorway service station and the table came up to her chin. I don't usually stare at abnormality, leastways not *openly*, but I'd never seen anyone so small. Her head was normal size, though, even on the big side, and she was glaring back at me pursing her purple lips and that furious colour said *fuck you*. Her hair was a black velvet curtain and those oriental eyes were hard coal diamonds. But her arms and hands reaching up over the table were the size of a china doll's. She was grotesque, repulsive and utterly beautiful.

Etienne's voice was soft-pitched like the sad notes of a concerto you'd strain to hear, but hope you'd miss because you know they were going to break your heart. The first time I heard that voice, this is what she said:

"When men stare like *you're* staring they're wondering how it *is* with me."

She leaned her head back like it was too heavy for her neck and she closed her eyes. Then she snapped her head upright again and asked me, sweet and low,

"What's your excuse, my friend?"

"I think you're amazing," was all I could say. At that time, I said exactly what was in my mind.

She nodded, lifted her cup (preposterously large against her little hand) and I lifted mine, like a toast.

We clashed cups and out of the corner of my eye I could see men circling like vultures, thirsting after Etienne.

"Well then," she said, "here's to *us*."

It was Etienne said we should steady the friendship washing through us like the waves of the ocean, make it last. One night on, one night off, she said and, in our lives together, we told each other about our lives apart. I'm a sub-editor on a technical journal owned by a construction firm in Cologne. Before Etienne, there wasn't much to tell but Etienne's wide-eyed listening coloured every detail of my life red and shining. Etienne was an auctioneer with a London Antique House and her life was sequinned with excitement.

Etienne's parents (*normal size, you understand – I'm a first-generation freak*) had been killed by a tornado in Colorado, their camper lifted clean up, shaken, and dumped down in the middle of a freeway two miles on.

"I'd gone across the park with the trash," Etienne explained, "turned round and there's this black tornado coming up fast on the van."

26

She lowered her voice to a theatrical whisper.

"I ran after it and it turned *thick* red. Thought it'd sucked the blood out of my mum and dad, thought I could catch the blood in the trash can, pour it back into them."

I gasped.

"Turned out to be corn poppies torn up from the fields."

And we laughed and smoothed out Etienne's white satin chair-covers and I drunk in every word of every adventure that she told me.

She'd swum for her life in the eye of a storm off Mexico while the sea all around her boiled malt black. Hiked across Yellowstone when it smouldered with fire and lodgepole pines exploded like Roman candles. In Brittany, she'd driven her Mustang right into the Pont de Terenez ravine (*why?* she didn't say *why*) and survived. "Only one who ever did but the Mustang got beat up pretty bad."

Maybe Etienne had a lover on her nights off but she was never specific about that. Some evenings she was angry, striding across her purple carpets, way past her ankles in the pile. Sometimes she'd say this to me:

"They don't *know* me. They don't know what I am *really*. Just want to see if their dick'll fit." One evening, she confided,

"They get close enough, I'd *show* them what I am. I've got it tattooed on my thigh. Four letters, *there*," Etienne pointed between her legs. "Get in that close, they'll *know*."

I'm not proud of what comes next so I'll keep it short, get it over with quick. It was one of our nights off and I'm in a wine bar with this man who meant the world to me before Etienne filled my mind. The place is sweat and smoke and Jesus, I'm lonely, and I'm looking to leave and suddenly there's *Etienne* herself strutting in, gift-wrapped in red satin and wearing high heels like scaffolding and she's about waist-high to the man she's with. Now she's seen me and she's winking and the whole world's staring.

"You *know* her?" my man asks and like water from a storm

drain I'm telling him what I know about her, the red tornado and Yellowstone Park and the Mustang.

"You *believe* all that?" says my man looking round at his friends lining the walls, and every one of them's staring down at Etienne.

Now they're all laughing and I'm embarrassed and that's why I'm turning round so Etienne can't see my face and I'm saying,

"No, of course not."

Etienne's man's lifted her up so she's perched on a bar stool, legs dangling like they're over a precipice. Guess I'm seeing her as she really is because there's a cold cave opening in my mind and the word *tawdry's* sneaking out of it, and Etienne's magic's fading from me like a rainbow from the sky.

I'm pulling the box into the middle of the room. It's big but it isn't heavy. Can we agree to forget that business in the bar? Etienne never knew about it. I reckoned her life couldn't be up to much, least I could do was go on seeing her one night on, one night off like before, hide my impatience with her stories and look like I believed them, not go asking for *proof*. I *understood* and I kept her happy: I didn't know things were going wrong for her somewhere else.

Some taxi driver carried this box up to my flat two years ago. Etienne followed behind and asked him to wait and then she said to me, business-like,

"Got to go. Look after my box. I'll send for it."

I asked her why and where?

"Australia," she said and then she added, in the sweet and low voice I'd forgotten how to love, "always up and go when there's wounds to lick. Need a few months licking time."

I wanted to ask who hurt her but I didn't so Etienne carried on speaking and the last time I ever heard the music of her voice, she was saying to me: "Call me, I'll hear you. You know I've got the power, don't you?"

Yea, yea, the power. Whatever.

28

After ten months of nothing, I got in touch with the Australian police and they didn't care too much and took their time but they did track down a tourist who'd seen a dwarf answering Etienne's description swimming near the Great Barrier Reef. He only saw her for a few moments and then all he saw was empty ocean. Truth is, he didn't know what he saw and so the official verdict was: *missing, believed eaten by tiger sharks.*

Last night, my man wakes up, sees I'm out of bed and I'm sitting on the floor by this box and the moonlight's stroking my shoulders. He comes over, squats down, takes my hand and says gently, oh so gently,

"Reckon *Etienne's* in that box."

No she's not, but *something* is.

"Open it," my man says to me, and he's rubbing his face into the back of my head.

"In the morning," I tell him and I follow him back to bed.

Have I told you what the box looks like? It's the size of a tea chest but it's cardboard and Etienne's sealed it all around the edges with brown tape. There's a picture of *Rule Britannia* on one side in red and blue and a black hand and a white hand holding a dove on the other side. I don't know what it contained in the first place. This is the box that's in front of me now and it's morning and I'm standing over it with a kitchen knife in my hand and now I'm cutting through the brown tape and I'm lifting the lid.

I'm looking in and the first thing I release is the smell of our nights together: cannabis and Etienne's honey candles. Now I'm feeling around and there's not actually much in this box: seems like there's only two things. One's a scrapbook and under that there's a folded blanket. The scrapbook comes out first and I'm sinking to my knees and opening it. It's full, really full, of press cuttings stuck in and now I'm shaking and trying to keep my eyes steady. Here's one with the headline: *Le Miracle.* I can read French and I'm reading about Etienne surviving the fall into the ravine and there's a picture of her beside her beat-up Mustang.

29

And here's one about Etienne's swimming off the coast of Mexico in the storm – and here's a cutting about her parents' camper van snatched up by the tornado. I spend more time on this one because I keep reading the bit about the midget with a huge head chasing after the tornado with a trash can in her arms. And there's one detail Etienne got wrong. It wasn't corn poppies coloured that tornado red: it was geraniums. Red geraniums.

And it's now a photograph gets loose from the scrapbook, falls into my lap. It's a polaroid of me laughing and it reminds me of that night in the bar. Oh sweet Jesus, it *is* that night in the bar – there's Etienne in red satin perched on that stool. Why did she go keeping *this* one – you can see I've been drinking and I've got red eye – when there's masses of other photographs of us together?

And I'm reaching in again and there's this blanket and that's *it*. What can I tell you? Every word she said was *true*, apart from the corn poppies, and I'm turning to ice with shame. Looks like I'm never going to find out the other things – who hurt her so bad she went away and what that tattoo said – that word which said what Etienne really was. And I'm sure as hell never going to find out where she is.

I pull out the blanket. It's woolly and shades of ice-cream pink and I've seen Etienne curled up in it evenings when she wasn't happy. Guess it's Etienne's comfort blanket. I open it out, spread it on the floor and looks like she's scrawled something on the blanket with her purple lipstick. Smooth out the area round the letters and it looks like the word *tall* but that doesn't make any sense to me so I can't be sure.

I wrap myself in her blanket, draw in the thick smell of her perfume, her cigarettes and Etienne herself. The warmth of the blanket's beginning to melt me and it's now I start to talk out loud to my friend, beg her to come home.

Martin Malone

Winner of the 1999 Fish Short Story Prize

BBC Radio 4, BBC World Service and RTE Radio have broadcast my short stories. Supplementary Prizewinner Bridport '98, Hennessey Award Finalist '98, Francis MacManus Award Prizewinner '98. Published in Canadian journals, *The Fiddlehead*, and *The Malahat Review*. A Runner-up in Fish Short Story Competition '97.

Come to me, Sweet Dementia

Martin Malone

Passing the Japanese Gardens, the tourist buses parked liked elephants in an elephants' graveyard; old dears, old queers, old geezers adding to my already overburdened time schedule, padding across the road in front of me, soaking in every smell of every bonsai tree that that Japanese bastard planted in the National Stud years ago.

Tooting the horn doesn't work with these foreign tourists. I got a silent 'go fuck yourself Sonny,' from an elderly Canadian woman, and a middle finger up from another grey-haired doll, who I thought looked dead in her wheelchair. So I don't beep the horn. Unless they're old men, then I beep like crazy. They just glare at you, wishing they were 20 years younger so they could punch in your windscreen, and kick the bollocks out of you.

Five minutes late. The kids in the back don't give a shite. They're late for school. Kids hate school. They don't give a fuck about school. I don't know why I do, but I do. Shouldn't matter a wart on a cow's hole to me whether or not they take the education – but they won't turn around in 20 years' time, and accuse me of not seeing to their learning. Not that they'll be here. They'll be off in America or God knows where else. Driving the bastards over there over here. In their bucket-loads. Touring the Emerald Isle, looking for leprechauns, pony trapping in Killarney. Most of them will be old folk, or early retired folk, a reach beyond middle age. The sort who buy a pint and look at it; a pint of black beer with a white head, wondering if it'd foul up their pipe-works, leave them with rust in their knickers or boxers. Those Canadian old dolls – waving their maple leaf flags at me. Jeering. If I wasn't in a hurry – there's no telling what I'd do.

The teacher says nothing, but looks at her watch, and then the classroom clock. As though she never believed the time from a single source. Sorry, sorry. In a hurry. Look at me. Can't she see. I'm gone half-mad from the early morning rushing. Can't she see it in my eyes?

'Homework isn't being done, Mister Harris,' she says, voice like a robot on low battery.

'No . . . ' I take in my kids. Twins. Boy and Girl. Gina and Liam. Aged five. A minute between them, instead of the ten years I'd have preferred. I told them yesterday evening to get in at the table and do their homework. I told them. I was polishing their shoes, ironing their clothes, trying to fit a cup of tea in my mouth in-between. I mean, have I to sit down, and do the fucking thing for them?

Jesus, what is it about people? She follows me outside the classroom. A slim wisp of a thing. Black hair tied with red ribbon. Brown eyes that'd melt sugar. If I were ten years younger and not up to me bollocks in shite, I'd think about her in a way I haven't thought about a woman since the Royal Cow got up and walked off with a jungle swinger from Ghana.

'Mister Harris,' she whispers, 'may I have a word?'

Looking up and down the corridor I nod. She must mean with me.

She coughs.

'Yes,' I prompt. Be patient. You can make up the time later, boot to the floor on the M50. Why, a clear run might even see me on time for a change.

'The twins,' she says.

'Yes?'

'They're missing their Mum.'

Doesn't she think I know that? Do I look stupid? Does she think I look stupid? I didn't think I said that out loud, so I was surprised when she said, 'no, of course not.' Or did she say it. I thought she said it, which isn't actually the same as her actually saying it. Is it? I close my lips.

'Is she coming back?'

Everyone knows the story. Everyone knows that poor Paddy Harris's wife has left him for a black man. He has an unbelievably huge tool. That's what Moira told me. In a moment of spite, when I asked what had he got that I hadn't; apart from lips that threatened to engulf his nose and chin.

'I doubt it, Miss Clancy – she's having a really good time.'

'Oh.'

'Yes . . . yes. Size matters, Miss Clancy, believe me, with some women.'

She blushes in a way that I like to see in women. If we fell for each other, then she could live with me and the kids. It'd save me a lot of hassle getting in and out in the mornings – she'd be able to teach the kids at home. I'd be able to sit down and drink my tea for a change. I feel like telling her that I've had a vasectomy. But perhaps I shouldn't. Just yet. Shouldn't tell her I haven't had an erection since the op.' Sore balls, you see.

'Pardon!' she says.

Fuck. Must have slipped out. Why is that happening? I'd closed my lips. Maybe my ears have taken over the role of my mouth, or my arse. Perhaps it's a dual effort.

'I thought it was something you might like to know.'

Backing away, her arms folded across her breasts, I don't think she'd be on for falling in love with me.

Got to run. Across the yard, round the back. Run, run. I was a great runner in my day. I could run for hours. Being slow was my problem. Crows dining on waste that'd fallen about a wheelie bin, scatter as I breeze through them. Breathe in, breathe out, in through the nose, out through the mouth. Beautiful blue sky, not a cloud. Too nice to be stuck under factory lights, listening to a machine humming in my ear. Fuck the money. Who needs money? Go home, have a beer, maybe two. Clean up all last week's breakfast stuff. Catch the news on tv. Yea, factory smells; oil, and grease. Keep them. For today. I'll clock in tomorrow – the boss'll understand.

It'd only happen to me. A funeral. The slow roll of hearse leaving the grounds of the funeral home. A long and broad gathering of people walking behind. If it's not tourists, and teachers, delaying me, it's the dead. Rolling down my window I call an old geezer with stubbled chin and head, 'Hey Boss, who's dead?'

The old man stops shuffling, frowns, 'I don't know Sonny . . . but it's something to do, and the exercise keeps me going. Having company makes the walking easier.' There's some mad bastards in this World. I'd hate to be dead myself. I wonder sometimes what it's like, going to be like. Frightens me it does, the thoughts of dying. I wonder do madmen know if they're dead – I mean if they're not themselves when they murder someone, then who are they? And if they're not themselves when they die, then who are they? Who dies? I need time out to think about this stuff.

I'm thinking about it so much lately. My head feels awful hot and tight like someone with a big arse is sitting on it.

'Hey Missus . . . who's dead?' I call to a lady in black. Must be the widow. If she doesn't know, then no one else will. She just looks at me, and sobs, touches the rear of the hearse, as if telling the coffin that she was being bothered by a man, and her husband not cold in the sod.

After the church had swallowed the lot of them I pulled away. Heading toward the Japanese Gardens. I fancy a mug of coffee in the restaurant there, but not half as much as I fancy the young blonde who works behind the till. But she's way too young for me, and, but, it's no harm to have a look.

I should go home by right. Get stuck in and do the housework. But fuck it. Like. Everyone needs a little break. A little scenery in his life.

That horse which won the Melbourne Cup is here. Parked in a stall. He's a gelding. In a stud. Must be a right pain in the hole for him; listening to the stallions discussing the fillies they'd had. About the rides lined up for the next day.

Nothing but tourists here. A couple at the bridge feeding the swans and ducks. A crowd watching a stallion being led out. The blonde isn't working this morning. In her place is a mess with blue-rinsed hair.

Sipping at my coffee, I overhear the Canadian woman talking with the other; saying that if she'd stayed with her husband for another year, she'd have got his insurance money. The other saying she wasn't to know he'd die.

I must have said something, because they looked at me. I asked them what did I say.

'You know very well. I've a good mind to report you,' one said.

'Disgusting,' rasps the other.

'Jesus – I said nothing. Not a thing.'

'You must be mad, then, quite mad.'

That's when I considered the possibility – madness. All this rushing about, Moira running out on me, the pressure was finally getting to me. If I was saying things to people without my knowing, then I had a real problem. What if I started doing things that I wasn't aware of? Maybe I could hurt someone. One of the kids. A tourist. At this very moment I could be killing someone and I wouldn't know a thing about it. I could be making love to that blonde, and not know a thing about it. I could have a gun in my mouth and not know about it. Depending on others to tell me what I'd said and done is no way for a grown man to behave. Granted, the gun in the mouth bit – well, I wouldn't be alive for anyone to tell me anything. But the blonde bit. That's different. Unless I raped her, which I wouldn't like to hear about, or do for that matter. I need to see a doctor.

The waiting room's packed until I say and do something. People call me nasty things. Say they're going straight for the Gards. That doesn't worry me. I don't know what I said, or what I did. So I can deny whatever I'm supposed to have said or done. If it goes to court the Judge will let me off lightly. He will believe me when I say I wasn't responsible for my own actions. He listens to supposedly sane people who are found guilty of murder, and lets them free after a year or two. So, for a mad man, the prospects are promising. But I wouldn't go round murdering just anyone.

There are those who need to be culled from our society . . . like the old, the very young, the sick, the mad, some breeds of dog, and more of cats. Cows. A few horses. Black men. Not all black men, just those with big tools. Which could very well mean all black men. Cheating wives. Kids who don't do their homework. Kids who do too much homework. About the only thing in this World I couldn't kill is an honest politician.

'Mister Harris!' The Receptionist. What an ugly woman. All nose. Or is that a surgical mask? 'The doctor will see you now – seeing as everyone else is gone.'

I shrug, but again I must have said something, because disgust filled her eyes.

Her eyes are green, the colour of a swamp's.

'Close the door behind you; sit down, good man,' the doc says. He hasn't looked at me once. A grey-headed doctor, but not old.

'So what have we here?' he says, in a deep voice.

'Your surgery.'

'I mean what's wrong with you?' His lips pout in tolerant amusement.

Wrong with me? He can't tell by looking? Well, things aren't as bad as I thought. I think about my kids. Who's going to be there for them when they get out of school. Sometimes I forget to collect them, and they've ended up at Moira's. I go mad when they

38

whinge about coming home with me.

'My wife fucked off on me, and I've been feeling down.'

'Do you have any suicidal tendencies?'

'You mean like wanting to kill myself?'

He has a lean serious face. His eyes squint up, as though he were squeezing someone's piss out of them, 'Exactly.'

'No. But I feel like choking the shite out of a lot of people. I'm sick of them. That bitch fucked off with a black bastard, and left me high and dry with two kids. I'm working in a factory that I hate. On shiftwork doing shitwork. And now there's fuckers accusing me of saying things I didn't say to them, you know?'

'I don't, but tell me.'

So, I tell the dopey fucker everything, and he keeps nodding and scribbling, and shaking his head. I expect his head to fall off and roll across the table. Does he do all this nodding and shaking at home? He should get something for it. Either that or pretend he's trying to invent a new dance.

He sighs, then says, 'I want you to think very hard, but say nothing. Then I'll tell you if you said anything. Okay?'

What's okay? That I understand what he's saying, or it's okay that if I talk without knowing what I'm saying? But I do it. I think awful hard. I squeeze up my brain, and boy do I think hard.

I think about that bloody black fella and Moira, and her begging for the kids to come live with her, and me telling her to fuck off, and that my kids aren't going to live under no black man's roof. And she saying I'm mad, that I could hurt the kids, and me going madder because I would never hurt my kids, and madder still because I think I could hurt them, and wouldn't know about it until I read the paper. Maybe my brain's like a lottery inside, soon as the right numbers fall I'm going to do away with a lot of people.

'Stop there.'

I study the doctor. He's joined his fingers in a steeple. Either to pray or to stop himself from wanking. You wouldn't know with some doctors. I'm going tell him to make sure to keep his hands on his desk, where I can see them at all times. If he's going to wank he can do it out in the open, and not under his desk like a pervert.

'You mean to say you don't realise you've been speaking to me?'

'Was I at it again? . . . fuck, tell me exactly what I said.'

And he did. Did he read my mind? Don't be silly, don't be mad.

He holds up his hands, slides back his chair. He's gone all nervous. I'd say the little weed's afraid of me. Are my kids afraid of me, too? They go awful quiet in the car when I start singing. I sing out loud, sing out strong, like Pavo whatever his name, 'Figaro, Figaro . . . Fig a Ro.' I used to think the kids loved it, but maybe they don't. Next time I'll twist the rear-view mirror and get a look at them as I sing. I suppose it's ignorant for a singer to sing with his back facing the audience. If I frighten them I'll shut up. But who knows, they might actually be clapping. Fuck the road in the front of us, it's wide enough for other cars to miss us, if they want to.

'Mister Harris, are your children coloured?'

'Are you getting at me? How was I to know she was going with a black fella? I put it down to genes or something. She swore she was never with anyone else only me. Lying bitch.'

'Mister Harris.'

Bitch.

'Mister Harris!'

Bitch!

'MISTER HARRIS!'

'What?'

'You are a coloured man.'

'Pardon – fuck off. Show me a mirror.'

He gets me one. He's shaping himself up like a sprinter wanting to get a good start. A round mirror in his hand shows me a black face. Not so black, just a light brown, not even that, if I look hard it's more of a tan, look harder again and I'm almost white.

40

Fucker doesn't know what he's on about. But then I sneak a good look. I'm black. Black Irish. Black. Now why the fuck would I think I was white. I guess, well, I guess I do need a little help. Nothing much; just tighten a screw to stop me spilling my thoughts, and fix up whatever brain cell thinks I'm white. A brain service. I can get it done when the car is getting his in the garage. Grand.

Well. I'm here. In a place where the windows have bars to keep out the World. Moira says I'll find who I am in here. The Doc says I'm getting better. I don't know about that. Looking through the bars, at the full moon, I think this is quite a pleasant place. There's no rushing about, no worrying about things. The moon relaxes me. I love its silvery glow. I just hope no one minds my howling. Come to me, Sweet Dementia – I'll be dead and won't even know it.

Is wanting to go mad a sign of madness?

'It is.'

Did I say that?

Patrick Sandes

Winner of the 1999 Fish Short Story Prize

South Africa was my birthplace and home until my parents decided I was altogether too comfortable and that a boarding school in England was indicated. After school, I spent two years training horses in Spain and several more as ne'er-do-well in England and Ireland (barman, farmhand, statistician, whipper-in to a foxhunt, and dockyard labourer). I eventually left for Canada en route to who-knows-where, but found it much to my liking.

So I stayed, took a degree in English, and after several more false starts, resumed my erstwhile calling in training . . . this time people rather than horses. I've been at it ever since and, after twenty years or so, believe I'm getting the hang of it. So much for my "day job"; I write at night when time and energy permit.

Reptiles

Patrick Sandes

The boy is on his knees, locked in stillness, focused on the sleeping yellow snake which lies curled in concentric rings under a bush. The sun is directly overhead. The bush with its few leaves offers scant shade. At some distant point of consciousness, the boy feels the sand biting into his bare knees, the sun searing the skin on the back of his neck. The hot air vibrates with the song of insects. Heat and sound unify the boy, the bush, and the snake.

The obsidian eyes blink open and stare at him. A bead of sweat rolls down his neck. His breathing slows. The black tongue slips from between rigid lips and the forks taste the air. The boy is deathly still. The snake raises its head an inch, moving it up and back, appraising him.

The cobra's body, a pale, gleaming yellow, thicker than the child's wrist, is a concentrated weight, solid upon the earth. The boy wonders what sits within the flat, diamond-shaped head, what thoughts and feelings flow there. He knows in his bones that in that precise, concentrated coil of muscle, thought and action are one.

The tongue flickers out again, its tips playing like fingers on the air. Then the head lowers and rests on the top coil once more. The boy breathes out, hearing the air whisper in his nostrils, the tremors in the taut muscles of his back. The hot bite of sand beneath his knees is fierce now. But movement is a problem. He feels the exquisite balance in the situation. His mind, in the aching stretches between seconds, explores the paradox: stillness – and staying – are safe; movement – and leaving – are dangerous. The cobra knows.

It occurs to him, in another of those abysses between seconds, that it will be lunchtime soon. He may be late. His mother's face, her voice, disapproval more terrible than snakebite make his heart lurch. A surge of feeling courses through him. The feeling is so violent that he imagines the cobra will take fright and strike. It does react, even though he has not moved. It raises its head again, a little higher this time, a little quicker. The boy holds his breath, feels the beating of his heart and a soft pounding in his ears.

The bell, a couple of miles off, behind the house, will soon send its meagre clang across the veldt. The farm workers will turn for home. Liza will waddle back down the hill to her kitchen, singing Xhosa songs of love. The maid, Jane, will carry lunch down the long hallway to the dining room. Mother and father and brother will draw their chairs to the table. And his place will be empty. She will launch an inquiry. Blank stares will answer her.

The cobra holds its position, its head still and sure on its column of gold. The tongue touching the air, the black eyes focused. The boy's heart is pounding. He knows the snake sees clearly, can taste his fear upon the air, is certain of its superiority. He feels an infinitesimal easing as the snake's head moves slightly from side to side.

Lhosie's words come to him. They'd been talking about Xhlobindula, the blue-headed lizard that lives under the step, that the boy had been trying to befriend. "He is a god, mThalashushu. You must see him first and then he will come to you. To see him truly is to love him."

He looks at the cobra, its head is still swaying slightly, its

44

tongue working, maintaining its watch. He looks into the cobra, not past it, not just as far as its skin, but into it as Lhosie has taught him. He feels a drowning in the connection between his eyes and his heart. He feels a warmth growing in his heart, like a flush upon his cheek. It wells up and spreads outward. The beat in his ears slows and disappears. The cobra's head lowers. The great tide of song from the insects washes back over them.

The boy lets a long breath out. He wants to stretch this moment now, but the seconds are chiming with the cicadas. He knows that bell will ring. With his eyes and his heart focused on the cobra, he plans his movements. He will have to rise up on his knees. This may come as a threat to the snake. First he must get it used to movement. He straightens his shoulders slowly, watching the cobra all the while. In his heart now, the force of love is so strong that he has an urge to reach out and touch the gleaming scales. He is certain the cobra would accept him. Instead he moves one arm slowly, bringing it out to rest on the ground. He leans his weight upon it and shifts his balance, easing his legs out sideways beneath him. The snake is still. The boy uncoils himself and stands. Then he walks away.

A short distance off, he turns. The snake lies as before, watching, then it slowly glides out, first towards him and then off into a promising stand of cactus. Liza's bell tolls and the boy jerks into a desperate run for home.

They are seated when he sidles to his place. The curtains are drawn against the heat of the day. The room is shadowed and silent. It is slightly cooler than the world outside. Across from him, the brother's face hangs bland and blameless. The father is a silent presence to his right, barely visible. He feels her presence, like a hot lamp, to his left.

He rests his eyes on a little ceramic vase of petunias in the center of the table. They are purple and blue. He wonders at the heart that can conjure such beauty and also such misery – each with so little: a touch, a tone. Jane's careful body moves around the table, her face dark and expressionless. She puts a plate in front of the father, the mother, the brother and, finally, the boy. Curry. He can see hated onions and squash beside it. His heart sinks deeper.

"Where have you been?" she snaps.

"Out by the kopjies." His voice is thin and breathy.

"You've got dust all over you! That's no way to come to lunch. Wash your hands and face at once."

The silent reprieve of the bathroom, the water cold on his face, the glad gurgle in the drain. But there is no time to enjoy it. He feels her impatience reaching down the long hall. A grab at the towel, rubbing face and hands, noting with another dart of fear the dirt transferred to its white folds. Out of desultory talk of her horses and their performance that morning, the dining room falls silent as he pads to his chair.

"That took you long enough. Now get on with your lunch."

The lunch sits as he left it, the vegetables now cold. He pushes a fork into the curry, raises it to his mouth and swallows quickly. He clenches his mind to defeat the taste; it is hopeless.

"Sit straight!" she barks.

As he stretches his body erect he reviews the pitfalls ahead: knife and fork to be held just so, the fork in the absurd "correct" mode with the tines pointing downwards, the food balanced on the convex side; the correct alignment of utensils on the plate after it has been cleaned entirely; orange juice not to be swilled in his mouth (to defeat the curry) but sipped sedately; elbows off the table; back straight; worst of all, look at her when she speaks.

"What were you doing up by the kopjies?"

"I was looking at a snake."

"You were what? And look at me when I'm speaking to you."

Outside the house, he hears a mousebird squawk and a distant clatter comes from the kitchen. His heart is still, his body now of lead. It takes effort to turn his head, but he does it. His range of vision narrows to the tight pale lips, the tiny vertical creases on the upper, avoiding the eyes which can reach into him and turn his mind into dust.

"I was looking at a snake."

"What kind of snake?"

"It was a yellow cobra." The lips compress and the attitude of the face changes as she looks at the father.

"It was probably dead," the father says.

"No, it wasn't," the boy blurts, turning to the father. There the eyes are pale and distant. "It was sleeping. Then it lifted its head and looked at me. It was wonderful! And it didn't touch me."

"Nonsense," the mother snaps. She shakes her head at the father and brother. "I don't know why he concocts these stories," she tells them, then turns back to the boy. "Eat your lunch. I want to see that plate clean."

Something makes him look into her eyes. It may be the memory of the snake. They are a pale blue and they drill into his heart and mind, pushing back all he has to give. He drops his head and goes to work on his lunch.

There is a dull thud in his chest as he stolidly eats the squash, one cold clidgy fork-load at a time. He tries not to taste it, but it is hard and he fights the urge of his stomach to force it back up again when he swallows. In his peripheral vision he tracks the others' progress, thankful for the father's plodding work with knife and fork. The onions are slippery and sickly-sweet in his mouth, they slide down his throat and, again, he fights the reflex that wants to reject it all. An age passes, at last the plate is clean. To his right, the father's slow utensils come to rest. He calms a little.

"Sit up straight!" she snaps again, snatching the silver bell off the table and giving it a shake.

Jane wafts down the hall once more and puts the dessert on the sideboard. She gathers the plates, catching his eye as she leans to get the brother's. Her dark eyes hold him a moment and his heart eases.

Pam Leeson

Winner of the 1999 Fish Short Story Prize

I live in Manchester with my children Ed and Zhana, and write poetry, prose, scripts.

In Dec '96 my long poem *off white* won the Huddersfield Poetry Festival competition. In November '98 *Crocus* published *I'd ask and she'd nod* — a pamphlet collection of poetry. In Jan '99 *The Text* published *start with one eye open* — a short story.

(I am currently working on a collection of humorous biographies.)

the forces

Pam Leeson

she wanted to take off her stockings and let the waves fall over her toes, but the nails were painted red and she didn't know what he'd think.

he would have put his hand over hers at the point when everything went dark and her head was pulled back, and her watering eyes weighed up the size of the cloud that had covered the sun. but he couldn't be sure that was what she wanted, so he fidgeted and twitched and pretended he meant it.

when he said – what shall we do now?

when she said – what do you want to do?

she would have said yes if he'd asked her, but so far he hadn't, so she stayed quiet and listened to the sound of his breath as he inhaled his second cigarette, the smell too delicious not to concentrate on. she couldn't take in his explanation of· soap bubbles and the forces which mould them, of cloud formation, of the way the tide knows the time. his smoke-rings and silence disappeared up her nose.

he would have liked to pull up her skirt just one more inch as she leaned back and stretched, so that he could see if he was right about the width of her leg above the knee. he considered doing it accidentally.

when she asked if he was hungry she regretted saying it straight away, he was obviously happy to stay where he was. straight away she wanted to say I've changed my mind, let's hang on a bit.

he wanted to say have anything on the menu, don't worry about the cost.

when the waiter put the list of desserts in front of her she didn't refuse, even though the thought of cream made her feel sick and there was nothing that would taste good without it.

he desperately wanted another cigarette but he didn't want her to think he was nervous. he ordered a coffee to appear sophisticated.

she wanted to say no, she didn't like the taste, but that would have meant him drinking on his own, and orange juice was poncy.

the cinema was almost empty because of the sun. there was plenty of room to sit near no one. she went to the centre where there was chunnering and crackling, pretended not to notice the back row, where she wanted to go.

he had the chance to say no when she said was here okay.

she could smell the sweat from his hair mixed with the scent of his neck. she wanted to press her nose into the skin just below the collar and lick.

he could see a couple of inches below the neckline, her breasts squashed up. he wanted to pour popcorn down the front of her dress and pick it out with his teeth. he bit hard into the cardboard cup.

when he said – what shall we do now? she wanted to say let's walk somewhere where there was nobody else.

when she said – what do you want to do? he wanted to get down on his knees and wrap his arms round her waist and pull her thighs into his face and sniff through her skirt. he wanted to press his cheek onto her belly. he wanted to say let's go for a walk somewhere where there was nobody else.

when they were on their way up and the carriage juddered, she wanted to grab onto his arm and look into his eyes and say this is it.

when his stomach reached his neck and her screech reached his ear he wanted to shout I want to fuck you from behind while you pick flowers and thread them together and pretend to not notice what I'm doing.

half way through her scream she heard him think that he loved her and she wanted to say that she felt the same way, but she couldn't be sure it was him and not the bloke behind.

when she said – what about the waltzers? he wanted to say I'm spinning enough and the chips are churning with the coffee and the cake and I might be sick on your shoes at least.

when he said – sure, she wanted to say I don't really want to I was just saying it because the guy doing the spinning winked at me on the way to the big dipper, and I want him to spin us and watch my

51

skirt riding up, so you'll notice him noticing my skirt riding up. so you'll think about my skirt riding up.

when the gypsy man was looking up her skirt he wanted to press his hand down on it hard and feel her pubic bone through the flowers.

when he didn't notice the gypsy man looking up her skirt she wanted to pull his hair at the back and twist his head towards the gypsy man and say I want you to be like him, I don't want you to ask.

when she was obviously disgusted with the way the gypsy man leered up her skirt he wanted to say no when she said – shall we stay on?

when he didn't notice the gypsy man looking up her skirt, she wanted to grab his hand and wrap it round the flowers and make him pull it up.

when the gypsy man was looking up her skirt he wanted to press his hand into it and stop it flying up and shout to him, *I've* not seen it yet, *I've* not seen it yet you bastard.

when he said – yeah, she wanted to say don't you care that he's looking up my skirt? don't you want to leave this shitty pathetic fair and be on your own with me?

when she suggested staying on for one last spin, he wanted to slap her in the face.

when he said – yes, she thought he couldn't possibly fancy her and winked back at the gypsy man.

when she winked at the gypsy man he wanted to whisper – slag – in her ear.

when she got off and he didn't hold out his arm to steady her.

when he said he felt sick.

when she didn't seem bothered.

when he couldn't find the car.

when she asked for a cigarette.

when he started to hum.

when she kicked off her shoes and put her feet on the dash.

when he mentioned her toes.

when she mentioned the time.

when he mentioned the gypsy man.

when her face went red.

when he stopped the car and lit up another he wanted to say there are things that are good and things that are bad.

she wanted to say there are things that are real and things that are not.

he wanted to say there are some I will never remember and some I will never forget.

she wanted to say she wanted to be the first and she wanted to be the last.

he wanted to say that he wanted to cry when the gypsy man looked up her skirt.

she wanted to say that the gypsy man's eyes were a piercing blue.

he wanted to say that the gypsy man was dirt and grease.

she wanted to say that the oil-stained jeans of the gypsy man would stay on her skin so she'd never forget.

he wanted to say that the gypsy man's mother was the sister of his father.

she wanted to say she wanted to rock in the gypsy man's caravan.

he wanted to say there were murderers amongst them.

she wanted to say that the risk was the fingers and the thrill.

he wanted to say he would keep her from harm.

she wanted to say don't ever be my brother.

he wanted to say she had eyes like his sister.

she wanted to say she was a virgin.

he wanted to say he'd heard stories that excited him.

she wanted to say they were rumours, just that.

he wanted to say he would spit on the gypsy man's shadow.

she wanted to say that the gypsy man's eyes were a piercing blue.

he wanted to say that the smoke from the gypsy man's caravan was just the remnants of burnt-out fat.

she wanted to say that the smoke from the gypsy man's caravan was the friction of his fingers.

he wanted to stand at the side of the road and look.

she wanted him to see nothing but her.

he wanted to walk out of her view and feel some relief, but there was nowhere to go that wasn't too far.

she wanted to look away, but something made her watch.

he wanted to say that the rumours were true.

she wanted to say that she was a virgin, but the side of his face was tightening in time to the lights on the road and the colour of one sock was different to the colour of the other.

he wanted to say that the light from the outside made her look different.

she wanted to say yes when he asked her to listen, but the noise of his voice and the laugh from the lips of the gypsy man stopped her hearing.

he wanted to watch her cry in her sleep.

she wanted to sink her feet into the sand but her toenails were painted black.

he wanted to touch her elbows and knees in public.

she wanted to say what he wanted to say.

he wanted to hear it in public.

she wanted to stay in the light.

and he wanted to stamp on the gypsy man's shadow.

she wanted to agree, give her permission without saying a word.

he would have asked her to submit.

she would have stepped out of her shoes and leaned her head back and held up her chin.

he would have left the lock on the door, watched her struggle with the mechanics of the seat belt, but there were things that were genetic and these were included.

she would have opened the gate and stood to the side.

he would have stiffened his arms and strided more inches.

she would have picked up the paper that flew by her feet that was torn in two, but she wasn't sure if they went together.

he would have swung round his keys like it was no big deal and say what he wanted to say. that his father.

56

she wanted to say that her mother.

he wanted to say that his father had never threaded his belt through all of the loops and his mother had always been smaller than him for all of his life and the grin of his brother would loom up through the bedclothes and the death of his sister had never affected his love for her. and that the whole of his childhood was a thing of the past.

she wanted to say that her favourite record was something too obvious and her favourite dress had been worn by her mother and that her father left words that could never be fathomed. and that her very first kiss. her very first kiss. his lips didn't fit.

he wanted to say the way her mouth made the shape of a triangle.

and that her very first boyfriend went to live in the woods.

he wanted to outline her flowers and rub out the gypsy man's eyes.

she would have let the water fall.

he would have put his hand over hers.

she would have let the water fall over her toes but the nails were painted a piercing blue and she didn't know.

Scott Lipanovich

Winner of the 1999 Fish Short Story Prize

has lived all his life in northern California where he hikes, fishes, and complains about suburban sprawl. He has worked as a roofer, freelance writer, and for many years, in a college library.

Scott's stories have appeared in a variety of publications, including *The Seattle Review, Crosscurrents, Abiko Quarterly, Gold and Treasure Hunter, The Good Life, Ridge Review, Summerfield Journal*, and several anthologies. He has written a children's book, *Ice Chief: The Life of John Muir*.

He does not steal from construction sites.

Aqua Linda

Scott Lipanovich

After dinner Mom and my younger brother went over to Aunt Flo's. My dad went next door to help Mr Maher pour cement. I was in the den watching the Giants game.

When my father came in, he leaned over and clicked off the TV. Thickly set, he had rounded shoulders and a whitish, bald head. His long nose, kind of a ski-slope, was bent out of shape from several fractures. The tweaked nose was all that remained of his short career as a boxer after World War II.

Dad said, "I think you'll get a kick out of this. John Maher's up to his arse in concrete." In his right hand was a flashlight. He said, "Come over and hold the light for me."

My inclination was to stay put, because I'd reached that age when it seems essential to make parents work for a response. However, my father didn't smile like that often. It made me curious, and I followed him outside. The sky was milky with overcast, the night air cool on my arms.

In the Mahers' yard were lawn chairs, a ringer washing machine, a rabbit hutch. We stepped around a large concrete basin. Meant to be a fountain, this was Mr Maher's previous attempt to make use of the electric cement mixer he had picked up cheap from some guy in a bar. Mr Maher saw me. He slipped a pint of whiskey into a back pocket of his dark slacks.

I was disappointed. I had expected to see him sloshing in

59

concrete, like a pig in mud, though I have to say he did have wet patches all over his slacks and shirt.

Mr Maher was an embalmer. His hands were stained a filmy yellow-green. The joke about his drinking was he embalmed himself more than the corpses.

His glasses flashed as he looked at my dad. "You brought one of the gremlins," he said.

Dad said, "You're gonna need all the help you can get." He shined the light across a glistening plane at the base of the wood stairs that led down from a laundry porch.

Mr Maher said, "I'm telling you, Roy, this stuff's like elephant shit. You can't *control* it. Maybe we should throw some dry on her."

Dad clicked off the flashlight. He handed it to me. I noticed how patient he was with Mr Maher, and patience was not a quality you would normally associate with my father. He said, "It just needs to set up. Now get me that hacksaw, would you?"

The yard was ringed with cherry plum trees, but once your eyes adjusted it wasn't very dark back there. Dad picked up a hammer, stained with concrete, and cleaned it by rubbing it across one of his work boots.

I looked around. The square form was about half filled. I said, "You can see all right. You don't need me."

Dad said, "I might need your help down at Aqua Linda. You never know with John."

"Aqua Linda? I don't get it."

Dad said, "You heard me. Aqua Linda."

That was the name of a swim club being built at the bottom of the hill. My parents were against it. They said it would bring too much traffic to the neighbourhood.

I said, "Oh, that's real clear."

Mr Maher hummed as he came toward us. He said, "Here she is, Roy. Got a new blade on her."

The three of us stood together. Mr Maher's breath stank of whiskey.

60

I said, "I still don't understand what you're – hey, I just got it. You're going to steal something."

"The word is liberate," my father said.

Mr Maher said, "Don't worry, gremlin. They won't even notice anything's gone."

My dad, Mr by-the-book, was going to steal something? This I had to see. Still, I feigned reluctance. "Why should I go if I don't know what we're after?"

Dad said, "We found the Lost Dutchman's Mine. It's in that big pit down there. Now come on. And keep your voice down."

He led us to the back corner of the fence separating the Mahers' yard from the Pluffs', the next family down the street. Behind the Pluffs' yard began the field that ran to where the new swim club was going to be. Mr Maher started climbing over the fence. His shoes thumped against the boards. Dad webbed his hands, to give him a boost, and the Pluffs' German shepherd started barking.

Mr Maher let go, dropped to the ground.

Dad whispered, "I hate that goddamn dog."

Buck was the neighbourhood terror. In dogfights he went for the throat. The previous summer he had charged out at Jay, my brother, who was riding his bike, and knocked him over. Jay's chin had required three stitches.

Buck's harsh barking rose in pitch. Someone inside shouted his name. The three of us were hidden, squatting beneath a bulky plum tree.

Mr Maher whispered, "One time he wouldn't quit unless I turned off the radio. I'd turn it off, and he'd stop. I'd turn it on and he'd start in again. I got so mad I got out the B-B gun and shot that donkey."

Dad said. "You should've used a twenty-two."

There was a gulping sound. Belching, Mr Maher said, "Should've used a hand grenade."

Dad said, "I'll supply the hand grenade. Just let me know

when."

Dad's father had been a drunk, the kind who liked to work off his failures by beating the shit out of his wife and kids. He had been run over by a car, in 1947, and his existence, like the war, was simply not talked about in our house. With Mr Maher, however, who was fifteen years older than Dad, drinking made him friendlier. When absolutely smashed he loved everybody. He and Mrs Maher didn't have kids, and I know these circumstances contributed to Mr Maher and my dad's friendship. Hiding in the dark, waiting for the dog to quit barking, I was filled with a giddy elation. It was like joining a club.

Inside the Pluffs' house, someone shouted, "Buck! Be quiet!" This time he was quiet.

Dad said, "Let's give him a minute to settle down." He was resting on the balls of his feet. He tapped me with the saw. "If John don't put rebar in that patio, he's gonna get cracks. So we're going to take some from where they're going to build a retaining wall down there."

Mr Maher said, "Gremlin, I wouldn't let you do it if it was hurting anybody."

Dad said, "Shut up, John. Have a drink."

We picked our way down through blackish humps of coyote bush. At the bottom of the hill were stacks of culvert pipe, a trencher, a grader, and a metal trailer that served as an office. At the end of the new road leading out to Keith Avenue was a chained gate. In front of it were sandwich boards topped with blinking yellow lights.

It didn't take long to find the booty. I held the flashlight while Dad took four steps from the end of a bundle of rebar at least thirty feet long. He sawed in the same way he did everything: intensely, frantically. He cursed under his breath when the saw jumped the cutting groove. He got halfway through one, worked it back and forth over his knee, and snapped it. He cut another. Mr Maher took a turn and Dad wandered off, looking for shorter pieces of rebar in need of liberation.

Mr Maher snapped one over his knee and said it was my turn. I set down the flashlight. I went to work – and swore when the saw jumped its groove. And I remember hearing myself sound like my dad, which is to say I heard how dumb I sounded, cussing at metal. I slowed my pace. The saw made a rhythmic, scraping sound.

Mr Maher took one of his deep, smelly breaths. He bent over, close to me, and spoke over the saw. "Your daddy, he was paratroopers and I was infantry, but we look out for each other. We always have."

Mr Maher straightened up, took a hit of whiskey. He gazed at the cloudy sky. I knew my father looked out for him a hell of a lot more than he ever had to look out for my dad, and this knowledge emboldened me.

I said, "Could I ask you something? Me and my brother have kind of a bet going."

Mr Maher made a waving motion with the pint bottle. "Go ahead and shoot," he said.

I said, "I was wondering. Uh . . . " I checked around for Dad. I didn't want him to hear, because though he often made fun of Mr Maher he was also protective of him. I saw Dad over by the pit, where the main pool was going to be. I managed to get out: "My brother says you put underwear on the dead people for funerals." Mr Maher sighed; it turned into a blustery belch. "Well, gremlin," he began, "the family usually brings in a whole set of clothes for the big day." As he talked Mr. Maher leaned – sagged, really, toward me again. His face was like a purple balloon. "So usually, yes. We do. But there's no inspection for that sort of thing. So sometimes, you know, I keep 'em. And whatever they came in with has got to go somewhere, too. It just needs washin', if you get my drift."

I got his drift. He bore in even closer. "*Hell*," he said. He looked down. "I think these socks came from Jack King. You know, King's

Nursery?"

By then I felt weird all over. My stomach was queasy. I tried to
not think about Mr Maher taking underwear and shirts and socks
and God knew what else off dead people and then wearing them –
and of course I couldn't think of anything else.

Meanwhile, Dad didn't find any short pieces, but he came back
with two lengths of wire. He quickly cut more rebar, and tied the
wire around the ends of our haul, eight bars. He and Mr Maher
each took a side and we headed up into the coyote bush. Mr
Maher was in front. I shined the light ahead, so he wouldn't trip.

He told a story about stealing an airplane while on leave from
Fort Benning, during the war, heading for New York and landing in
a fallow potato field on Long Island. Stepping over clumps of
grass, I tried to stop the dizzy laughter that had overtaken me. The
whole night was crazy: Dad stealing stuff, the tales. Mr Maher said
he had ditched the plane and hitchhiked into New York, where he
signed into a hotel as Dr Eyetooth, from Wisdom, Kansas – and
just then a low shadow streaked between the bushes, right at us.
At the moment I knew what it was, Buck bared his teeth, and
snarled.

I said, "Cool it, Buck. Be quiet."

Buck growled and swung his head, blocking our way.

A few feet to the right of me, Mr Maher said, "Don't move, he'll
bite."

Dad said, "John, set down your end and kick the son of a
bitch."

I said, "Take it easy. I get by him every day on the way to
school. Right, Buck?" His loud barking made me nervous. "I'll get
him to calm down." I tried to convince the dog, saying, "You'll calm
down." He barked one short, sharp call. I said, "You two go on,
before somebody comes, I'll take him to Aqua Linda and walk up
later."

Buck lifted his head, and snapped his teeth. Dad said,
"Goddamn it, John. *Kick* the bastard." Mr Maher said, "We better

keep it down is what we better do."

Buck took up barking like he had earlier, like he was warding off prowlers. I said, "Come on, be quiet. Let's go for a walk." I put a hand out. His barking got lower, stopped. "*Good* dog," I said. To Dad, I said, "Once you're past, I'll walk him the other way."

Mr Maher started up, his shoes crunching grass. My hand tested the air between Buck's snout and my fingers. He sniffed. The outline of his collar showed darker than his fur. As my father passed I turned and said I'd meet him at home – and Buck's snapping teeth grazed the back of my hand. Instinctively, I drew it to my stomach. My hand stung. Buck snapped again, this time at air, and Dad dropped his end of the rebar and kicked Buck like you'd punt a football. Buck flipped over.

This took not two seconds. I saw Mr Maher stumble, the rebar fall to his left, the hacksaw to his right. Dad's blocky shadow, hunched, moved forward. His bald dome glowed. Buck gained his feet and pounced. Dad's boot met his snout straight on.

Buck's teeth *clacked*. He hit the ground, wriggled to his feet, and Dad's boot knocked him over again.

Mr Maher said, "Hey, Roy, take 'er easy."

Buck got to his feet.

"How easy was he on Jay?" Dad said. He shot forward. Buck fell, his head swinging like a fish out of water. Gobs of blood flew from his snout. My father kicked him, one-two, one-two, one-two, like punches in a boxing match.

The blows brought a rising moan from Buck.

My brain was racing, but I couldn't get my feet to move. I opened my mouth. Nothing came out.

Mr Maher lurched by. He grabbed Dad by the elbow and pulled him back. He shouted: "That's enough!"

I hate to admit it, but rather than think of the animal I looked up the hill, to the back of people's houses.

Dad threw off Mr Maher, who stumbled sideways.

Buck rose. Dad jerked forward with another sweep of his right leg. *Thup.* I got a glimpse of the bloody mouth. A jolt of adrenaline sent me running. My right arm came down, a real haymaker. I slammed the flashlight into the top of Dad's head, then backed away.

Dad shook his head a few times. He reached up and touched fingertips to his bald head. There was a gash about an inch long. Dad licked his fingers and rubbed them into the cut. He said, hoarsely, "All right, all right all ready."

Dad turned around. I'd never seen him look shocked before – and rather than wait to see what might happen I sprinted up the hill, a broken yellow flashlight wrapped tightly in my hand.

I went to my room and turned on the radio. Mom was still over at Aunt Flo's. I kept seeing Buck's twitches, the gobs of blood. About half an hour later I heard Dad come in through the garage. He went to the kitchen. A few minutes later, the doorbell rang. Dad called out, "Get that, would you?"

I walked down the hall and opened the door. Standing three feet away was a blue-hatted policeman.

He said, "Is your mother or father home?"

With effort, I got out, "My dad's here."

"Could I talk to him?"

I spun around, glad to get away. Dad had heard this exchange and came out of the kitchen, wiping his mouth with his right hand. We brushed by each other in the short hallway between the entry way and the kitchen.

Dad said, "What can I do for you?"

The cop said, "I'm officer Thompson. I need to talk to you for a minute."

My father said, "Okay," but didn't invite him in.

By then I was at the kitchen's avocado-green formica counter. I was trying to decide whether or not I wanted Dad to get in trouble. Simply the idea that it could happen was intriguing as hell.

I heard the policeman say, "Do you know Mrs Pluff, from down the street?"

Dad said, "The Pluffs have lived there what, five, six years?"

Standing against the counter, I edged along it, so I could see down the hall. I noticed that the policeman's voice was steady, and that my father's voice grew slightly louder every time he spoke.

The policeman said, "Mrs Pluff called to report a neighbour found their German shepherd out on Keith Avenue. Said he looks like somebody clubbed him. Her husband ran him down to the vet."

Leaning to the left, I saw my dad. The hall light shone on his bald head. His jaw and crooked nose jutted forward enough to indicate he wasn't afraid. He put his hands in his pockets – and with relief I saw he had taken off his shoes. They would have been wet, and bloody. For some reason he looked smaller than usual, standing there in his bare white feet.

The policeman said, "Mrs Pluff says she let their dog out, and he didn't come back."

Dad's jaw rose, a fraction of an inch. He said, "I thought there was a leash law in this town."

"Leash law or not, the neighbour who found the dog says he heard barking and yelling out in the field behind Keith. Mrs Pluff says you and Mr Maher were in his backyard, mixing cement. I'd like to know if you heard, or saw anything unusual."

Dad shifted his weight from one foot to the other. Slowly, he rolled his neck, like he was stretching, like he was trying to remember if he had heard anything odd out there. As Dad's neck turned, I saw dried blood on it. The blood looked like a sticky fingerprint. It was most likely his own blood, from the top of his head, but I figured the policeman saw it too and would assume it was dog's blood.

Dad said, "With that cement mixer going, I couldn't hear much. You know? I'm still half dingy from all the noise. Did you talk to John Maher about this?"

"I tried," said the reasonable voice. "The lights are on but nobody answers the door." The cop didn't say anything for a few seconds. I was certain he was deciding whether or not to ask Dad about the blood on his neck. He finally said, "Basically, all I need to know is if you and your neighbour were really out there doing concrete work tonight."

Dad swung his head, again exposing the blood print. "Absolutely," he said.

"But you can't tell me anything about what happened down by Aqua Linda tonight?"

"If I think of anything," Dad said, "I'll call." They both said goodbye, Dad shut the door. I headed for my room. My father intercepted me in the hall. He pinned me with those watery eyes that didn't blink.

Dad said, "I want to make sure we understand each other."

"I won't tell anybody."

"I don't mean that." Dad wiped his bald head. He stared at me like he might never see me again. "I want to make sure you wouldn't do anything like this. Put yourself in this kind of situation. Right?"

I was twelve years old. I had new friends and a new school and was spending more and more time away from home. The whole world was changing for me whereas my father still woke up at night, sweating, seeing the faces of Japanese soldiers he had tortured during the war.

I walked away from him, to my room. Only then did I start shaking. I had seen the depth of his sadness and it scared me.

For years I ran away from this sadness. It was a part of our house, so I spent as little time there as possible. When I finally asked him, about the death of his father, and the war, Dad shrugged and told me to forget about it. My wife had recently had our first child and my father was more interested in the little guy than in explaining himself to me.

When I pressed him, Dad said, "I've paid for my mistakes, over the years. I don't want to go back – neither should you."

Graham Mort

Winner of the 1999 Fish Short Story Prize

Graham Mort lives in North Yorkshire where he works as a freelance writer and tutor; he is currently director of studies for the Open College of the Arts. His latest book of poems, *Circular Breathing* was published by Dangaroo Press and was a Poetry Book Society recommendation.

Why I've Always Loved Fishmongers

Graham Mort

I've always loved fishmongers. Ever since I was a child and stood in front of their windows in the town where there was a row of fish shops following the hill down to the market square. I love the red honest hands of fishmongers and their smeared white aprons. I love the fishy smell of them. And I love their thin, worn-away knives that are so very sharp. The way they slide them along the spine of a mackerel or herring. The way they lift the backbone clean out.

There's something infinitely treasurable to me about the grotto of a fishmonger's window, its cornucopia of the sea. And let me tell you, I hate the bloody mess of butchers' shops. The butcher is a crude mechanic by comparison with the fishmonger's artistry. He shows only parts of an animal, their ribjoints, loins, neck, legs, kidneys, livers and lights. But the fishmonger offers you the whole creature you're about to devour, head, tail and fins. Though they're dead on his slab you can imagine their lives in the rivers and the seas so easily. You can see them leaping from the phosphorescence of the fishing boat's bow wave or hurling themselves upwards over the sheet silver of a weir.

I love fishmongers and the clean, hygienic windows of their shops. Their piles of ice like the jewellery of a snow queen, their heaps of winkles and mussels and oysters with sequinned shells.

Their fans of herring and trout, skate wings and seabass, red and grey mullet, the fillets of hake and cod and huss, the fat coils of conger eel or the dull red meat of shark steaks cut from behind a staring savage head. Silvery mounds of sprats and sardines, sliced whiting and coley, hake and halibut and the slack gaping mouths of codfish. Lastly, the shells of live crabs or lobsters, those anachronistic war machines of rusted iron. The way they stalk blindly about their tanks, the armoured, predatory spiders of the sea.

Let me tell you that this is a love affair which will not go away. Each night I dream of fishmongers unpacking their crates of ice, lifting out the slender, delicate bodies of fish under the moon. Cradling them tenderly in their mercurial slime and bearing them away like lovers.

My father never touched me until I was eleven years old. Then we had a secret and my mother's eyes behind her spectacles stopped seeing. Let's be clear: my father was never a fishmonger and he disliked eating fish, though he spent hours trying to catch them. I remember him choking on a fish bone when I was very small, holding onto my little sister and watching him go blue as my mother pounded his back and the meal went cold. Whenever we had fish after that my mother had to search through it for bones and my father would search after her, probing it with his fork until we felt sick watching him. Sometimes it was cod or haddock rolled in bread crumbs and fried, but usually it was fresh grilled mackerel that my mother brought home from the market.

Much later, I remember my mother buying fish fingers and cooking them for tea. When my father came home he said, 'What on earth are these?' and when my mother explained that it was fish with the bones taken out he was delighted. It was a long time before my mother tired of the blandness of fish fingers and we had real fish again. Even tins of pilchards had a spiny piece of bone that caught in your teeth and had to be lifted out carefully from the little fish. I remember how the cat loved those bones especially, mewing like a crazy thing and rubbing against my legs with her ecstatic, hypocritical fondness.

Sometimes we caught sticklebacks in the stream below the house and kept them at home until the water went foul and they died, belly-up and stinking like the worst cowards. My father came to me at bedtime when my sister was safely asleep in the next room and my mother was busy over the ironing board pressing his white shirts for work. When he touched me it was like opening the pink gills of a fish and I caught the faint smell of salt water as if there was an ocean or estuary inside me. Afterwards I could feel it washing backwards and forwards. Backwards and forwards inside me like a wave over strands of slippery weed.

I've got a seashell here in my hand. Faintly pink with dull purples and blues. They lie sleeping in the rough surface until water lights them and they glint with memories of the sea. My little sister found this shell on the beach and gave it to me because I was crying over something. Because my father in his swimming trunks and long arms and hairy belly had got too close and hurt me. The shell whorls into a tunnel like the inside of someone's ear. I called into it for help or for sheer love of the sea where it swayed in green glassy waves. Inside the sea and inside me tiny fish were darting, silvery as those shoals of stars that turned the sky to milk at night.

I remember the first time I put my ear to the ear of the shell and we heard the sound of the sea in each other. The shell pink and clean as the inside of my body, gleaming when it was wet in a hundred subtle colours which I learned to call hues. He'd spidered his arms around me under the water where no one could see the hurt, just our heads bobbing like corks. It was no use calling out because everyone yells with cold or surprise when they enter the sea.

A fishmonger must lead a strange and beautiful life. Rising early from sleep to drive off and collect his boxes of treasure from the wholesale market. Inside them on the ice lie the closely-packed bodies and the blinded eyes of fishes. Or perhaps he rises even earlier, before the dawn is tingeing the sky. Driving all the way from our town to the coast, walking the quayside, waiting for the fishing boats to come home. Standing where the fishermen's wives wait fearfully near an angry sea. There he can chose from the open crates of freshly-landed fish, bear witness to the strange, deformed monsters that the sea has made inside itself. Deep down, away from the light that we take for granted but which never reaches the ocean depths. I can't bear the thought of a polluted sea, its poisons twisting the exquisite bodies of fish that gather there under the waves like dreams. Under the waves where the light of day is only a faint green glow. I can't stand the thought of what we're doing to the seas and long for the purity of salt water and wind and time passing.

I've seen my own body like that in other dreams. Tangled in a fisherman's net and dragged out from the deep with my long dark hair wrapped around my waist, my cunt salty with days in the sea, my nipples icy from the freezing water. Each time I'm hauled ashore onto the seaweed and shingle one kiss on my cold lips would wake me, but no one dares. Instead the fishermen gather and mutter in foreign tongues – Portuguese or Spanish, the unearthly vowels of Welsh or Gaelic. They stump around angrily in their seaboots, trying to make a decision until I'm thrown back into the breakers. Another useless deformity of the deep.

My father kept a fishing rod and a creel of bait and hooks in the garden shed. On Saturdays he went fishing in the canal after his week in the factory office where he added up the company figures and did complicated sums. Where he spent his days submerged in the teeming shoals of mathematics. Sometimes I or my sister or both went with, him staring into the water where the factory chimneys wobbled in wintry light. Down in his keepnet we'd see the pale flicker of a roach or the dangerous spine of a perch. Their lives so secretive, so different from our own. Their fixed stares, their mouths opening and closing, trying to catch something just out of reach or understanding.

Sometimes my father would take a small fish for live bait, dragging a hook into its body right along the spine, fixing it there as it writhed in his hand, choking on air. The scales would come away on his fingers and he'd wipe them carelessly on his thigh and go piking in the reed beds. I'd watch the poor fish fade and glimmer in the water until it died on the hook, its silvery gleam growing fainter and duller like an electric light flickering into darkness when the current inside it fails. Though sometimes there were monstrous pike stalking that glimmer, seizing it then being hooked on the end of the line. Dragging down the red-tipped float.

My father would play them so calmly and cunningly. Giving them line, deceiving them into thinking they'd broken free, then almost imperceptibly reeling them in inch by inch, foot by foot. Until he pulled their long, reptilian bodies from the water. Their ugly mouths lined with sloping teeth, dragged sideways by the cruel hook. Their bellies sagging and struggling and their goggle eyes glittering with an ancient greed. My father would drag them in with the gaff hook and finish them off on the bank with sharp blows to the head. He'd tell me how the female pike sometimes ate the male after mating and I'd gladly watch her striped body thresh at the end at the gleaming, almost invisible line.

One year at Christmas my father came to my room smelling of beer and cigarettes. He sat on my bed and told me a story about a lost boy. Long ago and far away in the Old World this boy had chased a runaway kid goat onto a mountain and then had lost himself as darkness fell. He'd heard the goat bleating and found it on a rocky ledge and stayed with it all night singing to it, hugging it for warmth and playing his flute until the moon had risen in the east to light the pathway home to his mother and his father, the goatherd.

Ever after, the goat had been his special friend and people began to think that the boy himself was only half human. His long hair was tied back with a leather thong and the notes that came from his flute were like the bleating cries of a lost kid. When a drought struck the village, withering all the crops, the villagers suspected the boy of sorcery and decided to cut his throat to end their bad luck. But as the angry mob surrounded him and as the headman raised his knife, the boy bounded away from them in the shape of a goat and was never seen again. As my father told me the story I thought of the boy's wicked yellow eyes smiling at me through his words.

After the story, when the goat-boy's eyes faded into the darkness of long ago, my father touched me for the first time so that I wriggled like a fish and loved him for it and would keep the secret forever. My mother would never understand our love even though she slept with him and knew his warm tobacco and sweat smell, the touch of his lips and rough cheeks. Sometimes I thought about her breasts and I envied them above all else. The breasts I didn't yet have. I imagined them iridescent, like fish scales in the moonlight under the song of the little goatherd, imagined that this was what drew my father to her bed when he left me each night. Kissing me on the forehead and asking me to promise never to tell. Yet I'd seen the fishmonger in his shop letting his knife slide into the belly of a fish and bring away its head and guts, slicing it all away as if nothing mattered.

Never is deep and final. It rolls in your head in waves that get higher and higher but never break. That day at the seaside I had sand in my nails and he touched me clumsily under the water and hurt me for the first time in my blue swimming costume. Perhaps not meaning to, under the water where no one could see. Just two heads bobbing in that swaying green and the sun glaring on white cliffs and the gulls screaming close, telling everybody who would not hear. That day I found a huge crab on the shingle and dropped a stone onto it, smashing its shell. All week it rotted and stank in the sun and I felt such terrible guilt that I'd killed it. Years later I realised that it was already dead, already scuttling along the floor of some ghostly ocean, its pincers stretched out to grab whatever mortal prey was there.

Some nights I dream of nets wrapping around me like wet hair, of my father's drowned face found under the canal bridge where the tench swam, deep and secretive – a long fish with thick rubbery lips. My father has never caught one, his clever hooks sliding empty in water which was shaken by traffic, which reflected the sky. Rain broke those pictures of the world above the canal, pelting onto the surface when they found him near the lock's falling tons of water. My father wanting to be a fish, wanting to breathe dark water instead of air, his fingernails torn off from so suddenly leaving life. Or from finding out that he was not watery-lunged or cold-blooded or fishy enough to live in that sly, suffocating element. *Never* is a word without depth or fathom. I wanted them to throw him back into that trembling water-sky to try again. But my mother kept his body in the air and blubbered over his blue face and salted it with tears.

Now I have a glass of water in my hand and on the plate in front of me are three sardines fried quickly in olive oil with a handful of green capers, seeds of the nasturtium. I've dashed the vinegar bottle across them and squeezed out a yellow crescent of lemon. I eat them with slices of German rye bread and mouthfuls of spring water from a source in Scotland where the rain still runs pure over the granite and heather of the moor. I picture this with each mouthful of hot fish, each time my teeth meet and crush their fried bones.

Today the fishmonger smiled at me as he looked up from filleting a brown trout on his cutting block. He threw the guts away and held its skin in his hands and smiled at me and I knew that he was thinking of the countless shoals of fish that dart in rivers and rivulets and oceans. I knew that in the night he would dream of fish as I would. Their golden eyes, their mouths bulging with the purest water, their gills coaxing out its difficult oxygen. That was a trick my father never learned and trying to learn it cost him his life. That the fishmonger had learned it I knew for sure. He'd smile the same

77

smile as each gleaming fin stroked his face where he lay staring upwards through weed and water at a thin moon polishing the pebbles of the river bed.

Tonight he and I will glide from saltwater ocean to the river's mouth. We'll swim upstream to the foaming edge of a waterfall, smelling out the peaty stream where we were born together as sister and brother. Tonight my breasts will stand out, cold and taut in their nickel skin of fish scales and I'll arch out in ecstasy, leaping above the ocean and the river to fall back gladly into their depth. I'll leave salt water for fresh, swim in the milt of my lover's sperm, letting out orgasms of fabulous jewelled eggs as his flanks stroke mine. No fingers or panting breath or hot skin, no secrets to keep or lies to hold. But coming again and again with this wild electrical pleasure, the shuddering beauty of his touch.

I count out silver coins from my purse onto the fishmonger's hand. The irises of his eyes are pale grey, the colour of watered silk. I give him the exact price of the fish, coin by coin. The fishmonger smiles and turns to his window, tipping a bucket of mackerel into trays of ice, lifting a salmon reverently onto its watery throne. The fishmonger's wife comes to the doorway and scowls, watching us together as if she knows everything. But the fishmonger still wears that secret smile as I put the sardines into my shopping bag. Wears it again as we say goodbye. I turn to go and a lobster waves its claws, troubling sediment and sand in the tank where it waits to die, wafting up tiny pebbles that sway and slowly sink again.

I've only told you half a secret, because the rest is unsayable because no one else can really understand and perhaps they don't even want to listen. They pursue their own lives in the streets, in factories and shops and offices. In cars and in suburban houses where the curtains are drawn at night and televisions blare, blinking blue light at the walls of their living rooms. They go on, day after day, night after night. Immersed in sitcoms, in stultified marriages, in children who call out for attention from upstairs rooms. Look how the hall lights come on. Look how they leave half-hearted conversations, or the news half-watched, to go upstairs with soothing words and hands. No. They need never know what we know. The fishmonger and me and other water-breathing dreamers.

Ian Wild

Winner of the 1999 Fish Short Story Prize

Lives in Enniskean, West Cork, with his wife and two children. He's currently writer-in-residence in Tig Filí (Poets' House). He wears clean socks everyday and has been accused of having a sock fetish. He is editing *Poets for the Millennium Anthology* for Bradshaw Books and currently has a play touring Co. Cork called *Somebody and Nobody*.

The Woman Who Swallowed

The Book Of Kells

Ian Wild

The day that Freya swallowed The Book of Kells was quite eventful. Travelling back to Cork on Iarnród Eireann, she'd had some difficulty in concealing the fact that her stomach was sticking out at weird angles under the skin. She told an old man opposite that she was having a triangular baby. Talk about indigestion! When she belched, the air stank of old vellum. On reflection, she regretted hitting two security guards with a crowbar, but it was that or eating photographic facsimiles of the original. The taste wasn't the same.

Her oral fixation with religious texts started at the age of six when she had been made to eat Old Testament passages dealing with Sodom and Gomorrah for saying *Shit*. Her parents had a talent for imaginative punishment that comes only with genuine religious fanaticism. Freya was twenty by the time she discovered – to her dismay – that other sinners thought eating bibles was *weird*. By then it was too late. She couldn't kick the habit and she had developed a connoisseur's palate where religious texts were concerned.

It's fashionable these days to blame the parents, but they had only been doing their best. When every evening their daughter told them she was going upstairs to pray, they never thought for a moment that she was actually using these long hours of solitude to nibble at stolen religious tomes like an enormous mouse at a block of cheese. Freya would lie on her bed and gnaw, eyes bloodshot, mouth foaming, until she got an almighty rush from this frenzied mastication. The only trouble was, the longer she went on, the rarer were the manuscripts she had to devour to get a buzz. One thing had led to another until . . . well, The Book Of Kells had just seemed too mouth-watering to leave alone. Maybe it *was* an irreplaceable item of national heritage and of incalculable historical importance, but so was the potato, and people were always eating *those.*

When Freya arrived home from Dublin, her parents were arguing as usual. They hardly noticed her going upstairs, they were so busy throwing plates at each other. Once in the sanctuary of her room, Freya stripped off in front of the mirror. The book was taking a long time to digest. Her stomach still looked as if she'd swallowed a pyramid side-on. She knew she would have to lie low for a few days until the whole coloured manuscript had travelled the long sausage of her intestines. No clothes she tried on could adequately hide the bulge. She would have to feign illness. If her parents got a close look at her abdomen, they would assume she was pregnant and probably have her kneecapped by the local priest.

Freya was in bed when her parents finally looked in.

"You alright, girl?" her dad asked, a huge shard of ceramic still sticking out of his head like a broken satellite dish.

"I've got a bit of a funny tummy."

"Its all those beans you eat," said her mother with the sympathy of a firing squad. *"There isn't a single line in the scriptures about eating baked beans. God's probably put a curse on your blasphemous stomach for not sticking to loaves and fish."*

Her dad said: *"We just saw on the telly. Someone's stolen The*

Book O'Kells from Trinity. Isn't that terrible?" He sneered: *"Yer mammy thinks that God fancied a read, but when he put his big hand down to get it, he knocked the two security guards flat."*

"I did not say that."

"You did! How could ye explain it otherwise? Would it be Christian fer God to knock 'em on the head on purpose?"

"T'would if they were sinners."

"Ah shut up, woman."

"I won't."

"Ye will!"

Another argument began. Her parents went into their own room where there were more painful objects to throw. Dad's fist came through the wall.

"Missed." jeered her mother's distant voice.

But the dysfunctions of Freya's family life faded beside the peculiar sensations caused by the religious toxicity of The Book of Kells. As Freya lay on her bed and stared at the ceiling, a hand holding a quill appeared and wrote: *initium.* The red word looked like it was drawn in blood. In fact drips of red seemed to appear across the plaster. Feeling distinctly unwell, Freya started to hear voices in her stomach whenever she hiccuped. The ceilings and walls had become a golden blaze of orpiment, and funny dogs were wriggling like snakes on the carpet. Then fish started to swim towards her over the bedspread. *Fish!* In early Christendom the fish was a symbol for Christ! It was time to crawl to the bathroom.

Fortunately, the argument between her parents was still raging – though now in an unfamiliar Gaelic. Shooing half a dozen peacocks out of the bath, Freya locked the door and sat on the toilet. It was vital that she kept calm. She'd heard Religion was the opium of the masses, but this was ridiculous. She picked up the RTE Guide from where her father had dropped it. Even this was transmogrified. It was all in Latin. Gay Byrne looked all flat with feet stuck out at right angles. The text was in dense black calligraphy. Then Freya heard angry screaming from inside the toilet. She'd started to poo little brown monks!

The drenched scribes chased her from the bathroom, shouting at the top of their squeaky voices – shaking fists that clenched miniature goose quills at her. No wonder her innards felt relieved. On the landing, Freya met her mother, who seemed to have lost a dimension and walked like Captain Pugwash.

"Mam! You've got a halo!"

Invisible angels sang in an eerie choir. Mam was too busy calling the last shots of her argument. She threw a copper pot into the bedroom. Freya heard it reverberate like a gong as it hit her father's head. Though everybody seemed to be speaking an ancient dialect, Freya could understand every word.

"Take that you oaf!"

She turned to her daughter.

"What are all these smelly little scribes doing all over the place?"

Then she noticed her daughter's belly.

"My God! You're pregnant!"

A posse of Lilliputian monks grabbed Freya's ankles.

"She's not with child!"

"She's with book!"

"She's a heathen!"

"She's swallowed a de luxe edition of the gospels!"

"She's swallowed The Book of Kells!"

Dad staggered like a cardboard cut-out onto the landing, still dazed from contact with the copper bowl. Both parents looked at their daughter's belly with horror. Aghast that their own daughter would be going to Hell.

"Freya!"

"You?"

The mammy fainted. Dad's two-dimensional halo went up and down rapidly above him, like an indecisive flying saucer trying to land. Kicking away the monks who were stabbing her shins with quills, Freya ran. Fortunately, her dad could only pursue her sideways.

Once she was out of the house Freya walked quickly down to the city centre. Everything seemed normal for a Friday evening. Except for the calligraphy street signs and restaurants advertising specials of wild boar. She thought that probably a breath of fresh air was all she'd need. It was merely a question of staying out until the effects of the swallowing wore off. Freya wished she'd never touched the stupid book. Maybe if she ate some kind of antidote it would help? A tabloid newspaper – *The Sun* or something. Maybe if she could make herself sick, the visions would pass? She stopped at Patrick's Bridge to stick her fingers down her throat. Then she noticed something which made her forget all about prodding her tonsils: Viking longboats were sailing up the River Lee!

There must have been twenty of them, rowing up from Cork harbour. People congregated on the bridge to watch.

"Is this part of the Arts Festival?" somebody asked nearby.

"Stupid waste of Corporation money! Think how much it must have cost to make them boats and costumes, and hire all those actors for the night. And there's people homeless on the streets. Still, its very authentic. They look fierce. Are they real bows and arrows they're . . . urrghh!"

The man fell over with a feathered shaft in his chest. The crowd started to scream and panic as huge blonde-haired warriors bearing axes surged up the riverside steps and hacked at astonished tourists.

Freya legged it down Patrick Street. Behind her, Vikings roared and smashed the front windows of Easons. Crowds ran past her, wailing, panicking, bleeding. From behind a telephone kiosk, she watched *Abrakebabra* being looted and ravenous Vikings emerging with huge hunks of meat on a spit. Hundreds were dead and dismembered before Gards in squad cars burst along Patrick Street. They'd barely stopped when axed windscreens burst like ponds getting bricked. Further down the road, the invaders were pillaging *Argos*. Vast muscular Norsemen came out loaded with colour TVs and Hi-fis.

A distraught Freya ran home. She kept looking over her shoulder, knowing somehow in her guts, that the Vikings had come for *her*. She needed protection, but the authorities would be appalled by what she had done. They'd give her life and get doctors to remove the book's remains by Caesarean.

Freya ran along her street, and she saw the front door of her house had been kicked off its hinges. Inside, the living room was wrecked. The telly screen looked like a newsreader had staged a breakout. But all the glass was *inside*. Religious icons had been yanked off the walls and snapped. In the middle of the carpet, the two-dimensional figures of her parents had been ripped to bits. Blood stained the floor like ink. Holding the disembodied head of her mother, Freya said:

"Mammy? What happened?"

Throughout the house tiny scribes had been squashed underfoot like turds.

In shock, Freya staggered up to her room, where on so many evenings she had secretly eaten psalms, hymn books, and tasty bits of Genesis. Her stomach was no longer angular and fat. It seemed the book had been absorbed, and had become part of her. A low, deathly choir was still faintly hanging on somewhere in the attic perhaps, but little men tugging each other's beards had vanished from the wallpaper. Crying blindly, Freya opened the door of her room and stumbled towards her bed. She knelt beside it, hands clenched in prayer. But a word lodged in her throat like a sharp bone. She could not utter the word: *Christ.*

Then from downstairs, she heard guttural voices shout: *"Freya! Freya!"*

She leapt over her bed, flattening herself against a wall. They had come for her! Expecting to be murdered or raped, she shrieked as a band of filthy Vikings entered her room and roared in triumph – raising their bloodied axes to the roof. But unexpectedly, the winged helmets bowed. On their knees, the pagans announced that she was their Goddess.

A few hours later, looking over the side of a longboat, with a heap of plundered washing machines, microwaves and exercise bikes nearby, Freya watched the sun set on a calm sea. Her warriors rowed, their bare muscles glistening with sweat. In Nordic song, they were creating the saga of Freya: *The Woman Who Swallowed The Book Of Kells*. It all seemed so inevitable. So right. And though Freya stared long and deep into the darkening waters, she didn't see one single fish.

Derick Donahoe

Winner of the 1999 Fish Short Story Prize

Derick Donahoe, a farrier and a farmer on Eastern Oregon's high desert for much of his life, is settling into middle age with an undertaking no less difficult and risky, that of being a writer!

Sal

Derick Donahoe

Wind drummed in his ears, the mane of the roan mare whipped his face as he raced in his dream with the herd of wild horses, line-backed duns chiseled from the desert, their thundering hooves the thunder of his mother grinding coffee against the wall of the kitchen downstairs and he knew he was already late.

By now his father would be pushing harness over the backs of Buck and Dolly, the pair of matched Belgians he'd traded for last spring. Finished with the milking, his oldest brother Tom would be forking hay down to the steers and he heard Gene splitting wood for the cookstove. He jumped out of bed, ducking automatically to miss the rafters as he pulled on his overalls, his boots. He felt betrayed when he looked around the corner at his brothers' empty beds. Just because threshing season was over. Just because he was the youngest.

Through the smells of bacon frying he clumped down the stairs into the kitchen. He expected a stern look from his mother; instead she smoothed his hair with a wet hand and sat him down with a cup of Mormon tea, hot milk with a teaspoon of sugar mixed in. "Sleep well, Joey?" This made him even madder. It was enough that his father had sent him off to bed early, that his brothers hadn't even bothered to wake him up.

"Yes ma'am," he mumbled.

"Next year when you're twelve," she said, stirring an extra half-teaspoon into his cup.

One more year and he'd be old enough to sit in on family meetings. Last night he'd tried to listen but it was hard to hear, except when Gene let out a cackle and his father said, "Be still!" And when Tom pleaded, "Please Father, let me do it," and his father smashed his fist down, "No!"

Ever since last month when the government horse buyer came through Tom had talked about joining the army. If he waited a year until he was old enough, the war might be over and then he'd never get to go overseas. He needed his parents' consent. That's what they must have been talking about when his mother shouted, "He's too young," and slammed the bedroom door. And his father said in a voice loud enough that she could hear, "A boy's never too young to learn to be a man." Gene let out a laugh and his father yelled, "Be still, damn it!" And still it was. So still Joey was sure they could hear his breath against the floorboards, until the door to his parents' bedroom clicked open and he imagined his mother as he had seen her so many times, watery eyes working to focus behind her tangled corrosion of hair. "You want him to be a man!" she said. "What **KIND** of a man?"

Piled high with kindling, Gene burst into the kitchen and dumped it into the woodbox next to the stove. Giving Joey a smirk, he pulled one of the longer sticks to his shoulder and fired it, "Bam!" like a rifle into the ceiling.

"Off with you," his mother scolded and waved him like a fly out the door. "Go help your father finish up the chores."

Joey hated Gene. How come he got to sit in on family meetings? He was two years older and could hardly read. He was always getting into fights at school.

Joey slurped his tea. "If Tom joined the army he could send us letters with foreign stamps." Like the yellowed letters with stamps of kings and queens at the bottom of his mother's trunk. Between trips to the pantry she'd kept a pair of skillets moving across the top of the cast-iron range and Joey's words stopped her short. She stood in the doorway with her tongue curled, as though a seed was stuck in her tooth.

"You heard last night?"

"I didn't mean to."

"And you're thinking that it was Tom, now, that we were talking about?"

His mother had a different way of saying things. He hadn't noticed until the day he heard kids mimicking her in the school-yard. Instead of saying, "Go out," she might say, "Now be gettin' on out with you." The way she did now. "And be bringing the cream from the springhouse on your way back."

It was Joey's job to slop the pigs. He thought of how much he hated them as he poured the fetid mixture of mash and skim milk and peelings into the wooden trough. It wasn't so much that he hated **them**. They were clean enough, given half a chance, and sort of funny, the noises they made and the way they ate. He just hated so much what they would **do**.

"Stay away from the hog pen," the children had heard a thousand times. But of course Joey hadn't, watching wide-eyed as the old sow snapped up one by one the family of baby chicks, the banty hen squawking and hurling herself at the hideously grinning face until it turned and ate her too. And always the stories: the old man who went out to feed the hogs one evening and all they found the next morning were his rubber boots; the young mother who left her baby asleep in the shade of a bush while she wandered off picking wild berries.

Joey was almost to the barn when his father came out the Dutch door and strode past him without a word. Joey's hand was on the latch when a high, thin voice called after him, "Son?" At first he didn't recognize it as belonging to his father, who turned, eyes wide and glistening, and walked stiffly toward him. His face was about to break when he spun like a military man and marched off, "Don't liniment Sal!"

Sal was the oldest mare on the place, maybe in the valley. Since a child in his father's arms, Joey had watched himself grow through his reflection in the mare's brown eyes. Kind eyes, his father said, ones with lots of wrinkles. On cold mornings Joey liked to stand within her warm cloud; he liked to watch her eat, to hear the rumblings in her stomach. Lately his body would tingle when he lay head to tail the length of her broad flat back. The smell of her soft muzzle was the sweetest in all the world.

Sal nickered from her tie stall as Joey entered the crepuscular stillness of the barn. His father always bragged that the big roan mare had brought the three boys up. She had, too, letting them prop a ladder against her out in the pasture and all climb on. She never spooked, not at snakes, not even at her first motor car. She saved Tom's life one time, bringing him home safely across the river during a flood. She was his father's favorite for hunting – she packed and wasn't gun shy – and for breaking in new horses, she would reach over and nip a brassy young gelding that wasn't pulling his share.

She murmured at Joey's approach and dropped her head for a rub. That's when he saw the shoes as big as plates, hanging over the top rung of her stall. "Sal," he said, "who pulled your shoes?"

"Father did." It was Tom, mucking out a nearby stall. He set his manure fork aside and came over. They stood looking at her swollen hind leg. "She still can't put weight on it."

"She can, too." Joey grabbed the feathers on her fetlock and yanked a front foot up, forcing her weight behind. "See!"

Tom placed a hand on his brother's shoulder. "She's not getting any younger."

Joey had heard this all his life. Heck, the past six weeks she'd been hitched with Buddy, the big black gelding, pulling the grain wagon to town. That was Joey's favorite time, when the threshing crew, buttocks greased to keep from chafing raw, finished loading the wagon with sacks of grain and he was free, nobody yelling at him to fetch water or telling him what to do the whole way to town and back. Sal turned her ears back when he talked to her, when he sang, and sometimes when they were out of sight, he'd crawl onto her back, grab hold of the brass hames and ride.

But last week in town a man yelled at him to back the wagon, something his father told him never to do with a heavy load. On the way back Sal had begun to bob her head. The next morning she came up lame.

"How come Father doesn't want me to liniment her leg?" he asked his big brother.

"'Cause he don't want to waste it," Gene called, letting loose a cackle as he sauntered down the alleyway between the stalls. He grabbed a horseshoe off the rail and yelled, "Ringer!", the younger horses shying as he pitched it half the length of the barn.

Tom chased him off, came back with the shoe and slid it chiming against the others. He went to the wall cabinet and got the black bottle of liniment. "That a girl," he talked softly to the mare as he took out the cork and rubbed the pungent liquid into her swollen hock.

"It's all my fault," Joey said. "If I hadn't listened to that man it wouldn't have happened."

Tom stopped and looked at him. He started to say something and went back to rubbing. It must have felt good because the strawberry mare set herself, raised her tail and plopped a steaming pile of manure into the floor gutter in back of the stall. Tom handed the bottle and rag to Joey. "That's right," he told him, "rub it in real good, all the way around."

If anything was sick, even a chicken, Tom knew how to make it well. All week he had helped Joey wrap the leg with a warm towel before applying the liniment. It opened up the pores, he said. After the army he was going to become a veterinarian. Vet-in-arian, Joey said, but his brother always corrected him and made him say it right.

When they entered the kitchen Gene was already at the table with their father, who crinkled his nose at Joey. "I thought I told you to leave off the liniment."

"It was my doing," Tom said. "It draws out the heat, it makes her feel so . . . "

"I'm not talking to you," his father snarled.

Their mother dished out the eggs and bacon and fried mush. "Joey," she told him gently, "you forgot the cream."

He ran to the springhouse at the base of the draw. It was his favorite place and he could sit for hours in the coolness, in the quiet. Sometimes he would come upon his mother alone there in the darkness, and softly close the door. The small sticky frogs barely moved when he lifted the cream jar from the shallow pool.

His mother was gone, no one looked up when Joey came back in. He barely noticed the 30/30, usually over the door, that now leaned against the wall. The table jiggled when he sat down, knocking over the single rifle cartridge that had been standing upright next to his plate. The four of them watched as the shell, as long as his finger, rolled in a lazy half-circle and stopped.

"What's that for?" Joey asked.

"I'll be roofing on the barn today," his father said. "Tom, you're to finish up the plowing over on the river. Gene, I want you to take the wagon back over to Trout Creek for another load of shakes." His bristled face swung to Joey. "You're the youngest, been with her the least number of years. Your job is to take Sal out to the far end of the hog pen and put her down."

"Not the hog pen!" Plates rattled as Tom slammed to his feet. His father did the same and the two stood gripping the table and glaring as the cartridge began a long, noisy roll and dropped to the floor. Gene let out a laugh and caught a backhand that sent him sprawling against the wall.

"It don't pay to keep a work animal past its time." Their father's heavy voice was even. "This way we at least get something out of her." His eyes went to Tom, who turned and charged out the door. They went to Gene, smiling crookedly as he picked himself up. They went to Joey. "Aim at the high point of a triangle between her eyes. She'll never know."

When he returned the jar to the springhouse, Joey opened the door to find his mother, who hurried out past him. She was on her way over to the neighbor's, she said. Her hens were coming into a molt and the McCords sometimes had extra eggs, though hardly cheap at eight cents a dozen. She was a little ways off when she stopped and came back. Her eyes pulled at him as she pushed a folded envelope into his bib pocket and patted it smooth. "You'll be sure Tom gets this. You've got to promise me now."

"I promise."

The sound of steady nailing came down off the barn. The pigs grunted to their feet and watched through squinty eyes as Joey, with the rifle in one hand, led Sal limping through the gate. Everything that came in through that gate had somehow to do with food, and now the pigs followed, sniffing the ground behind them as the boy led the 2,000 pounds of horseflesh to the back of the sweetly stinking pen. Overhead the nailing stopped, then started in more rapidly as the hogs gathered in a half-circle. The oldest sow moved in for a better sniff and the mare laid back her ears and switched her flaxen tail.

From her years spent hunting, Sal's ears came together when Joey thumbed the cartridge into the magazine. He levered the shell into the chamber and she raised her head and looked about expectantly. Joey's back arched as he swung the heavy barrel upward, he was trying to hold steady on the high point between her eyes when she swung her head and he found himself looking through the watery sights at the blurred image of his father. Kneeling on the roof with his back to him, he nailed even faster . . . bam-bam-bam, bam-bam-bam . . . then a hand was on Joey's shoulder and another took the gun and it was Tom, who kicked at the hogs and shot his father a look that kept him from climbing down off the barn as he led the boy and the crippled mare back through the gate.

Past the corrals and through the pasture and out into the

stubblefield they went. When they came to the newly plowed ground the walking got hard and Joey panted, "Where are we going, Tom? Let's you and me go away . . . you become a vet-in-arian . . . "

"Veterinarian!"

". . . veterinarian, and I'll be your helper. We'll go to foreign countries, we'll visit Mother's people in, uh . . . "

"Ireland."

"That's right, Ireland," Joey said.

Sal saw it first. Instead of hitching up to the plow, Tom had hitched the Belgians to the fresno and scooped a narrow trench out of the soft ground. Without breaking stride he led Joey and Sal into it, she dropping her head and giving a low rattle as the fresh dirt banks rose halfway up her sides. "Stand!" Tom told the mare.

By now their father was down off the barn and they could see something gleaming in his hand as he half-ran out through the pasture. Buck and Dolly whinnied from where they were tied in the cottonwoods along the river – Sal raised her head and was calling back when Tom, stepping behind his little brother, reached around and pulled the rifle butt into his bony shoulder. The last thing Joey saw was his reflection in the great mare's eye, the tiny figure of the boy reaching to pull down the gun. The deafening blast. The hollow thud of the huge head against the dirt as Sal collapsed like a marionette, eyes rolling up, her tongue lolling out.

Joey's ears rang. His shoulder hurt. He stood, nose bleeding into his mouth as his father came gasping up. He threw his hammer aside. "I'm sorry, I'm so sorry," he sobbed and enfolded his youngest son, rifle and all in his arms.

But all Joey felt was the envelope crushing against his chest. "Tom!" he cried. He grabbed at his bib pocket, "Tom!" The envelope fell with the rifle to the ground as he tore himself free and started to run.

His father stooped for the envelope. He opened it and took out the seven faded one-dollar bills. His eyes went to the house as he mouthed the words, "I hereby give my consent . . . "

"Tom!" Joey stopped running and cast wildly about. "Tom, where are you?" His eyes raced to his father, who stood looking beyond the team in the cottonwoods to a figure, wet to the knees, walking away on the far side of the river. "Tom!" Joey screamed with all his might. But his brother never stopped, never looked back and the father and his youngest son stood watching until the figure was broken by the waving heat of the day and was gone.

Shereen Pandit

Winner of the 1999 Fish Short Story Prize

Shereen Pandit was a law lecturer and political activist in South Africa before coming to Britain in 1986, where she completed a PhD and also taught law. She now lives with her partner and child in the UK. Since she started writing in 1996 she has won several short story competitions and has had many stories published in magazines. Last year she delivered the Dr Seamus Wilmot Memorial Lecture at the Listowel Writers' Week and did some reading of her work. She has completed a first collection of short stories entitled *Aloes* and is currently engaged in writing her first novel and a second collection of short stories.

The Imam's Daughter

Shereen Pandit

I stood at the window, looking over the deserted tarmac towards the gate. It was days since any uniformed children had come to school through those gates, lined up at those doors, walked along the corridors beyond my office door, to sit quietly working at their desks, gone out to chat or play in the playground, in the way which up to now had been customary in my school. The few students who had come in were not in uniform – or rather, they were in the uniform of the young, the ubiquitous jeans and T-shirts of their generation. They were student leaders and activists who had come solely to use the equipment room to prepare newsletters and leaflets for the evening's mass meeting. They too, had now left. I could no longer hear the hum of the photocopier and the other sounds of their activities.

From the first, I had told them that I did not want to be involved in what they were doing. So they went ahead and used the school's facilities without asking me for permission. As the boycott went on, they continued to use them without even advising me of what they were doing, as they used to. It was a strange relationship. On the one hand they were obliged to trust me sufficiently to use my school. On the other, they were not supposed to trust me because I was the head and I still kept the school open. I was not supporting the boycott. I had crossed the invisible picket line.

No teachers had come in either. Most of my staff supported the boycott. Those who didn't were too scared to come in, but they made sure that they phoned me. Those on strike did not. I knew that many schools and many head teachers were in the same position as I. I wondered if they too longed for a return to normality – the bell ringing in the morning and periodically throughout the day, the silence of the corridors denoting work, not desertion, not really a silence, more a quiet hum of activity of which I was proud. Did they too long for the return of the days when our kids were just kids, having adolescent fun and adolescent fears, by turn precocious and puerile, rude and respectful, silly and sensible, dependent upon the adults around them, but desperately trying to break free – but young, so young, and ours to care for and nurture.

These self-assured young adults who seemed to know exactly what they were doing and where they were going, who ran boycotts and called for strikes, who organised mass meetings and saturation leafleting, who spoke in fiery tones from public platforms – these were not the kids I knew. And I feared for them – they were too young to have so much responsibility thrust upon them – responsibility for changing a whole country, perhaps a continent. But if not them, then who? Us?

I sighed ruefully. They regarded us adults as for the most part being too inept or too cowardly to wage the struggle as they thought it should be waged. They despised me for closing down the school, but I had my reasons. They thought that these reasons were largely personal security, a desire to stay on the right side of the authorities, keep my nose clean, my career afloat. I supposed I should be grateful that they did not condemn me outright as a silent collaborator for not taking an active part in the struggle. Would they believe that I also kept my school open so that they would have somewhere safe to do all their business?

I sighed again. After today, they would have every reason to think the worst of me. They would think that I came in every day because I wanted to keep tabs on what they were doing for sinister reasons, not out of concern for them. But what could I do? I had no choice. Well, I thought, turning from the window, there was one more task I could perform for them, before I found myself totally outcast by doing what I had been instructed to do. I left my office and went along the silent corridor towards the equipment room.

As usual, it was a total shambles. An incriminating clutter of bits which had been cut and pasted for originals of today's newsletter and leaflets, crumpled-up copies which had been messed up by the copier. I wondered who they thought would clean it up. I wondered whether they considered that whoever cleaned it up might hand the lot over to the security police, or that the SB as they called them, might stop by themselves, as they would later today.

I was surprised to find someone still there. Gathering together bits of paper and straightening out the chaos, was the sheikh's daughter. I knew that her name was Nadia – she was my student, after all – but I always called her that in my head. The daughter of Sheikh Ismail, the politically active Muslim cleric who had, whilst in police custody, "slipped on a bar of soap" and died as a result, about ten years previously.

She didn't see me at first. My rubber soled shoes did not echo on the stone floors of the corridors, so she had clearly not heard me approach. She looked up from what she was doing, startled to realise that she was not alone.

"Nadia," I said quietly, smiling to reassure her that I intended no harm. "What are you still doing here? I saw the others leave quite a while ago."

I paused, remembering that she wasn't even involved in any political activity. She boycotted school like all the rest, but she was not one of the leaders, or even one of the key activists – not according to my well-informed grapevine, anyway. So why was she here at all?

101

She answered both questions. "I came in to fetch some books that I forgot last week, Miss. Then I saw the mess. I thought I'd just tidy it up a bit. Someone might come . . ." Her voice trailed off, her usually pale face suddenly suffused with crimson confusion. She'd said too much. I wasn't supposed to know what they were doing. I was the "someone" who might come. Did she think that I might report them? Had I sunk so low in their esteem?

"Yes, I know," I said, trying to keep the hurt from my voice. "I was coming in to clean it up myself. They leave it every day." I laughed self-consciously. "Good thing I'm here all the time, eh?"

She didn't smile. Her mother had once told me that she never did. When she first came to my school, her mother had come to talk to me beforehand about this quiet child, who had not smiled or laughed or cried since she was six years old – when her father had died. I had told the other children about who she was, and of course the staff, so that they would leave her alone, if she wanted to be left alone. But that aloneness had gone on for all the time that she'd been here. In time, the kids, even the activists, forgot who she was. They were just little children when her father died. The struggle had produced many martyrs, and more contemporary ones were the remembered and revered heroes of their young lives. The ones of the past were buried in the political era which preceded the current one, the one which they were convinced would be the final thrust towards freedom.

"Miss," she said now, "they say that the SB are going around to all the schools checking up on which teachers are supporting the boycott and asking principals for lists of teacher and student leaders. Is it true, Miss? Will they come here to check up?"

I felt the blood drain from my face. Did she know? I looked closely at her. No. My imagination was playing tricks on me. The clear dark eyes which stared up at me questioningly were devoid of any deviousness. The only emotion in their depths was their customary sadness. Should I tell her?

There was no need. Uncannily, she sensed then why I was

hesitating. "They've already been here." She stated the fact calmly, as though it were an everyday occurrence, not one which had nearly driven me insane for the past twenty-four hours.

I nodded, not meeting her eyes and then turning away completely, busying myself with tidying up. "They're coming back today. For the lists. One of teachers absent. One of student leaders."

"What are you going to do, Miss?"

"I don't know, Nadia. I just don't know." I stuffed papers into black bags as we talked. How could I tell her that I, her head teacher, in charge of 600 students for most of their waking day, entrusted with their education, with their futures, did not know what to do when faced with choosing between their future and my own, their families' sufferings and mine? How could I tell her that, whilst I was still hesitating about drawing up a list of student activists at my school, I had already prepared the list of teachers who had not reported for duty during the boycott?

She said, "They'll detain all of them. They already have hundreds. It will break the boycott. People will be scared. It will all have been for nothing – all the deaths and disappearances and detentions."

I squared up defensively to face her, "I have no choice, Nadia. If I don't do it, they'll take me. They'll close the school down. Even if I say that all the teachers were here and that I don't know who the student leaders at my school are, they'll know I've lied. What good will that do – one more martyr for the struggle? One more nameless hero to forget?"

I could have bitten off my tongue. Her father, I had often thought, was one of those forgotten heroes. The furore in the immediate aftermath of his death soon subsided. People forgot, life went on. Her mother had struggled to raise them by herself. I myself had only remembered who he was when her mother came to see me about her. Even now, with this new uprising, people like him were seldom, if ever, mentioned.

She was looking steadily at me now. "You are thinking of my father. Yes, I know that the movement soon forgot my father, but they are not the ones who matter. That's what my mother tells us. She says that the people did not forget and it was in them as well as his God that my father trusted to take care of us when he went to do his duty. Besides, times have changed. The movement is stronger now, the ordinary people are more involved." I bowed my head, ashamed of my outburst.

"Every struggle like ours," she said quietly into the silence, "has more heroes and martyrs than it can remember. It doesn't mean that the people don't care. It's just that's there's too much to do to stop and call the roll of heroes along the way." Her words rather than her tone admonished me, goading me into defensiveness again by the implication that all I sought was notice for myself.

"But I have a family," I said. "Who will take care of my children, my parents? The movement's failure to remember will mean that they'll go cold and hungry." The child wisely did not respond with the obvious answer that the people whom I would report had families too. They were far less likely to see them again if they were detained, than I was.

She let me down gently, offering herself as an inferior comparison, she of whom too much courage and sacrifice had already been asked, "Look, Miss, I don't want to be a hero either. I know that people here at school wonder that I am not like my father – a leader, an activist. That's because I'm frightened. But my time will come, my mother says. The time when I have no choice but to do what is needed. I tell her that our family has sacrificed enough. She tells me that my conscience will tell me when it is enough. Perhaps it is your time now to decide. The teachers and student leaders cannot be taken now. All of them are needed."

I was not offended by the implication that I, by contrast, was expendable. I was too intimidated by the choice which she had resurrected before me – a choice I thought that I had finally made

104

when the restless night came to an end and I rose this morning to type the list. We said nothing further, steadily clearing away paper, tying up black bags, putting things in apple-pie order. But in my mind raged the chaos that this girl, this mere child, had sown. The clarity which dawn had brought was stirred up again, muddied, dangerous.

"We've finished here," I said at last, suddenly tired and drained. "Go home now, Nadia. Please go home. They are nearly due."

She nodded. She did not ask who *they* were or what I was going to do. Instead, she reached up and kissed my cheek. Then she turned and walked out through the door, down the corridor, out through the front door. She never looked back. Had she really just come to fetch a book, to tidy up?

I closed and locked the equipment room. Then I returned to my office and picked up the list that lay waiting on my desk. I turned it face down. I did not want to remember the men and women on it. Where I was going, it wasn't a good idea to remember such things. I reached for my cigarettes and matches. I lit a cigarette, then put the match to the list, watching it burn almost all the way to my fingers before I dropped it into the ashtray. Then I sat down to wait for them, smoking quietly, calm at last now that the decision was taken.

The year or two that I was detained seems of little consequence now, save for what they taught me of barbarism and ruthlessness, but also of fortitude and comradeship. I came home to find that indeed, my family were well and well-cared for, despite the periodic harassment which all families of detainees experienced. Nadia had been right, then, after all. The people had not forgotten.

She must have finished school during the time that the boycott was called off for students to sit their matric exams. I was still away when she entered university and it was there that I saw her again, at a campus rally which I attended soon after my release. The movement was on the ascendancy then, its victory assured.

I was sitting with a number of fellow ex-detainees who'd brought me along. I didn't at first recognise the slender figure who rose to address the rally from the platform, but I remembered the steady calm voice which had kept me going through many dark and lonely nights.

Towards the end of her speech, with the crowd vociferously applauding her, she held up her hand for quiet. The sheikh's daughter had grown up to fill her father's shoes. The people respectfully fell silent.

"There are many here tonight who have suffered in one way or another for the struggle," she said. "I said to a woman once that the list of our heroes and martyrs is too long for us to call the roll at every stage, but tonight I ask you to do some small thing to show them and their families that we have not forgotten their sacrifices for us. Let us dedicate the closing anthem to those heroes and martyrs."

She hadn't forgotten, no, she had not forgotten us. And as she led the singing in her strong young voice, did I imagine it, or did she at last smile at me, that wise child?

Rebecca Lisle

Winner of the 1999 Fish Short Story Prize

My first story: *Tinckell, Binkkel and Belle* was about three fairies who
kept pet bees and lived in flowers at the bottom of my garden. Sadly it
has always been out of print.
I write every day and can nearly spell now.
I almost never look through windows.

Mr McInty's Special Window

or
Why little girls should not peer through windows:
a cautionary tale

Rebecca Lisle

Chapter 1: When we were little

Ali and I started young. We started with looking out of her bedroom window, which was high up, and looking down into unsuspecting neighbours' windows in the street opposite.

I'm sure people have got more precious. More secretive. When Ali and I were little, gates were left open, lights were on at dusk and curtains not drawn, hardly anyone cheated and had nets. Peeping through windows was easy for two sweet little girls. Which we were. Honest.

Chapter 2: Doll's House Windows

The best places for peeping were those squat, sat-upon cottages with sunken roofs and doors pushed up under the eaves. They had tiny windows right on our eyelevel, doll's house windows. Lean-out-looking-like-Snow-White-Windows. You know.

It wasn't our fault. Those windows were our size and not much else is when you're nine. Ali and I saw all sorts, looking through windows.

Chapter 3: What we saw

We saw cats curled up like shells. We saw a fat man wearing only a vast pair of Y-fronts, lolling like a beached yacht in front of his television. A lady asleep on the floor and a yellow dog asleep on top of her. Toddlers in playpens, and they saw us too, but they couldn't tell and only grinned and waved their dimpled fists at us. They must have thought we were some sort of giant pop-up toy.

Chapter 4: What scary things we saw

We saw a witch.

Well, we thought she was a witch because she had this horrible wart growing out of the side of her face. It was like a chicken's claw, yellow and spiked, just near her chin. She had long, long black hair and she was far too old to be allowed to have long hair.

She lived in a grey stone cottage, so narrow it looked more like a shed. It was a cottage from another time, sunken down below the level of the pavement. Then Ali said it was sinking down to the devil, to hell, and we knew she was a witch.

We peered in at her whenever we could, but one day she suddenly loomed out of the shadows of her room and caught us with our noses pressed against her dirty window pane.

She flung open the door and we ran, slipping and scrambling onto the higher ground, shrieking with terror.

Chapter 5: What the witch said

"Fuck off out of it!" she yelled as we ran down the street yelping and giggling and shivering with fright.

I never knew witches said things like that.

Chapter 6: Mr McInty's Warehouse

Then there was the dilapidated old building down by the fish-and-chip shop which was riddled with windows. There were remnants of pulleys and platforms and winches on the outside: gigantic rusty chains with hooks dangled and clanked against the walls. On the ground floor there were massive double doors where in the old days, carts went right inside.

We used to stand and gaze up at it, a monstrous tower touching the clouds. Every window was grey with dirt but just showing through, were piles and piles of junk as if fighting for a better view.

Mr McInty lived there.

Mr McInty was the rag-and-bone man. He never collected rags or bones, but old furniture and iron which he went on stuffing into his rotting old palace even though it was bursting at the seams.

His ground-floor windows were our favourite to look through in the whole town . . . when we dared. We had to wait until we knew he was out, clip-clopping along the street in his horse and cart, his dog beside him, his repetitive wail of : "Anyol'ra'n'bo?" ringing out down the quiet roads like an eerie foreign prayer.

Chapter 7: Dirty net curtains

The windows were so thickly encrusted and festooned with cobwebs that it was like looking through dirty net curtains. But it was always worth it; Mr McInty's rooms were a paradise.

Standing on the old stone trough we could see pyramids of dusty clocks, brass bedsteads, paintings of sheep, chandeliers, open cupboards – layered with books and boxes and papers – dressers with ornate pillars and mirrors that were so old they'd gone green and gold.

We were desperate to get inside, but Mr McInty always shooed us away as if we were some pesky animals. Besides, he looked fierce, with a big beetroot nose and grey stubble on his droopy jowls.

Chapter 8: The Dreadful Dare

One day we were sitting on the little wall outside his place, swinging our legs, chomping through the last of our chips, when it dawned on us that the big doors were open and there was no sign of the dog, the horse, or Mr McInty.

"Do you dare?" asked Ali, nodding towards it.

"I do if you do." I said.

We left it at that for a few moments as we chased the last crunchy bits round our chip bags and licked our salty, greasy fingers. Then:

"Come on," said Ali.

I swallowed, and looking over my shoulder at the great empty-eyed building, slipped off the wall and followed her.

The yard was grey with cinders and charred remains from old bonfires. It was littered with scraps of tortured metal, an old garage pump, a dead pram, wrought-iron gates, sinks and a bath full of green water.

It was easier to stare at all these things than look ahead towards McInty's.

Whether it rained or not, the scrapyard was always blotched with puddles. Ali and I had known for a long time that some puddles were dangerous; usually the shallow-looking ones because they were really deeper than the ocean. So we took a slow, circuitous route to the gaping, dark-mouthed doorway.

Just by the doors, the dog chain lay gleaming like a silver snake. The collar was still attached, but there was no dog.

I looked at Ali. Ali looked at me.

Chapter 9: We go Inside

We shuffled closer, staring into the gloomy inside.

"Mr McInty?" we whispered. There was no answer.

"Let's go back," I said.

But Ali was grinning. "Soppy! Come on!"

So, my heart flapping and somersaulting like a crazy fish, we crept in.

There were cobbles underfoot, black and slimy with oil. It was cold, colder than outside and densely dark like the deepest forest.

All around us the place heaved and groaned with dusty old furniture wedged precariously from floor to ceiling. It smelt forgotten and damp and dustbin-like.

"Let's go," I hissed.

"No. I want to see."

Chapter 10: Up the stairs

So we went on. Through a corridor made narrow by hundreds of paintings and chipped gilt frames stacked along its sides, to an enclosed wooden staircase leading to the floor above.

This was a real adventure, this was seeing upstairs in McInty's. This was brave.

I tiptoed up the stairs behind Ali, clutching her school cardigan tightly; the wool grew wet and scratchy under my fingers.

It was very dark and the air was thick and stuffy as if it had all been breathed before, second-hand, just like all the junk.

Chapter 11: What if he's dead?

"What if he's up here?" I whispered. "What if he's dead?"

It seemed exquisitely funny to think of Mr McInty dead and we snickered and snorted, pushing and falling against each other as if joined by tight elastic.

"Come on," said Ali at last, "this way."

Ali always did things, you see: we both looked through windows but she opened them too.

We crept round the landing and pushed open the first door: it was Mr McInty's room.

Chapter 12: Mr McInty's Bed

There was a massive bed; a mound of stiff grey blankets, rugs and a moth-eaten zebra skin. There was a cooker on spindly black legs, so covered in rivers of congealed grease and fat, it looked like an angular stalactite. There was a television, a table with cold fish and chips on it, a ketchup bottle, a wardrobe with doors hanging open, chairs, a brown sofa. We stared, appalled and fascinated, and then suddenly, horribly, the bed heaved and we saw Mr McInty.

I felt terror creeping up my spine like a great caterpillar, tugging at every hair on my scalp.

"It's him!" I shrieked and grabbed at Ali. "Come on!"

I pulled at her, but she didn't move. So I didn't either and we stood and stared at Mr McInty.

Chapter 13: Mr McInty's First Smile

He was smiling at us. The growly old man was smiling at us. There we were trespassing and my parents were going to be so cross, and he was just smiling and even holding out his hand.

He's dying, I thought. It was the only possible solution. But I didn't care, I didn't care if he died. I wanted to go!

Ali went towards him, stepping daintily over the newspapers and folds of rucked-up brown carpet. My fingers were frozen in an arthritic fist in her clothes and I couldn't let go and stumbled along behind her, tripping and trembling.

He looked at us with an odd, apologetic smile. I thought he was going to say he was sorry.

"You're the little girls always peeking through my windows, aren't you?" he said in a low, broken sort of voice.

Chapter 14: What were we doing?

What were we doing, standing there in our gingham dresses, our hand-knitted cardis, hair in neat plaits? What were we doing? I hated being so close. I hated the smell. It wasn't right.

"I'm glad you came. I was just thinking . . . Well, you like windows, don't you, so come over here, come and look through this," he said, pushing back the covers.

There was something tender in his voice. A gentle plea. And he went on smiling.

I still expected him to apologize and I was quite ready to say: "It's all right, Mr McInty. It's OK."

We crept nearer, right up beside his bed and looking down, saw he had a peculiar black box on his lap. It was like a specimen box from the lab, black sides with a thick glass top. "Look," he whispered.

Of course we did as we were told. We were obedient girls. We peered inside. And just like in the lab, there seemed to be an animal inside the box, a species of very fat, pale brownish worm. As we watched, it moved ever so slightly, as if it were dying and gasping for breath.

We looked up at him wondering.

Chapter 15: Mr McInty's Second Smile

Then I saw his smile. It was a horrid smile now, it was all wrong; it had started slipping off his face, it was a smile that he couldn't control, all lopsided and wild. I stared at his flesh twitching beside his very red slack mouth. It wasn't right.

Ali said something and it was enough, I let go of her, shrieked, and ran.

I tripped on the loose carpet and slithered over the papers. I bumped into the side of the door, nearly fell as I got to the top of the stairs, then started galloping down them. I heard Ali thundering along behind me but didn't look back.

"Go on!" she cried.

We clattered down the stairs squealing and crying and giggling too, and dashed out into the fresh air, gulping at it as if we'd been deprived of it for years.

We ran across the yard, scampering carefully round the puddles, scrambled over the wall and ran all the way home.

Chapter 16: What we did then

When we got home we drew the bedroom curtains shut, in case, somehow, Mr McInty might be outside, looking through our windows at us. We got into bed, pulled up the covers and giggled ourselves into weeping jellies.

Chapter 17: What Ali did next

And Ali paid him back for scaring us.

The next time he left his warehouse unattended, door hanging invitingly open, Ali sneaked inside and stole one of his old clocks. She just walked in, took the clock, and walked out again. I watched it all from the gateway.

"Serves him right," she said. "Anyway, this is a girl's clock."

She's still got that clock though she's grown-up now. It's on her mantelpiece and I think it's rather valuable. It's made of black marbled onyx with four gold pillars and draped over the top, is a voluptuous naked golden lady doing something rather extraordinary with another golden lady. They are both smiling.

Hugo Kelly

Winner of the 1999 Fish Short Story Prize

Hugo is a Librarian. He spends much of his time dealing with other people's books. Someday he would like to produce his own. Being short-listed for this Prize has compensated somewhat for the arrival of his third decade. Competitions to date have been his lifeblood. He hails from Westport, Co. Mayo. This is an important fact.

The Face in the Wallpaper

Hugo Kelly

That summer there is something wrong in the house. You wander from room to room searching through the shadows for a reason. The face in the wallpaper smiles then sneers and you have to quickly run away. You suspect that it knows. It knows everything. It knows you would love a watch. "What do you want a watch for?" it sneers. "You can't tell the time." "Oh yes I can," you say but it doesn't hear you. No one hears you. The delta of meeting rivers on the cracked ceiling hold your attention. If you close your eyes you can hear their Amazonian roar. The diamonds that live in the carpet dance around you if you stare without blinking for long enough. The stairs to the attic is dark and there is a smell of old clothes and of another age that seems less bright than your own. The skylight in the attic is your friend. Its rich light performs a cross section on the darkness inside, revealing its dusty entrails. You leave ugly, snot-green spiked chestnuts here and the warmth opens them to reveal their wooden, shining pearls. The white dot is an eye. Their touch is firm, yet soft, perfect. They are the meaning of newness. You save the best one to show to Mr Canning.

Mr Canning lives next door. He owns the American Bar. Everyone calls it the American. He has postcards tacked to the wall behind the bar. Impossibly blue skies gleam, wealthy high-rise buildings talk money, arc-shaped golden beaches curl into bright horizons, tiny bikinied women swim about their dog-eared edges. He asks people to send them to him. They are his window into the world he says. You love the bar and its certainties. The comfortable red, foamy seats that gently fart if you move too quickly. The smoky, sweet smell laced with the undertow of paraffin from the heater. The big, brown colour television throwing out images. The stuffed fox keeping guard above the bar, looking calmly into the woods. Here is the comfortable company of men. The easy conversation. The rattle of the till. The confident clinking of money. The crack of matches. The smell of pipes. In here there are no faces or no shadows. Out the back there is a shotgun. Best of all there is a round clock that you don't need to wind. It is from this clock that you have learned how to tell the time. Mr Canning taught you on a Wednesday after school. Sometimes Mr Canning sends you home. Other times he produces coke and crisps. Today he reads the paper carefully. You count to one hundred in fives for him. He nods after each number.

"You're going to be bright. You will be one for schooling. What's the capital of France?"

"Paris," you reply.

"Do you hear what the lad knows and him only seven?"

The men look up, momentarily distracted.

"He's a bright one."

"And tall for his age too."

You peer at the clock. "It's seventeen minutes past five," you say. No one hears you though. No more compliments. They turn their attention back to their drinks. Mr Canning turns the page of the paper.

"Isn't that Ritchie Ryan an awful bollocks?" one of the men says. He wobbles on the stool. He is drunk.

"Shsss. Mind," says Mr Canning.

"All this metric nonsense they're going on about. Soon we'll be drinking litres."

"Half litres," says Mr Canning.

"God you know what I think it's going to rain."

No one says anything. A tap drips. A man coughs. You take a piece of ice in your mouth and crunch it. Rain is as inevitable as silence.

The man perched perilously on the high stool suddenly shouts out, "If it wasn't for the Irish, London would still look the way Hitler left it."

Everyone lifts their head in surprise at the raised voice.

The proclamation is too much and the man falls from the stool. "You bloody fool," Mr Canning says. "What time is the bus at?"

The man grunts. He is pulled to his feet by some of the fussing men. His lips are foaming. "Give me a baby power."

"I will not. You'll go easy until the bus."

"Just one. Good man. I'll leave you alone then."

"No more you'll get here and that's for sure."

The man stares at him. His eyes travel across his face. He has bad teeth. He needs to shave. A rim of dirt is cut against his neck. He picks up a shopping bag and nearly falls over.

"You bloody fool," Mr Canning says.

A damp patch forms about the man's thigh. You can't believe it. A grown-up wetting his pants. You never would have thought it was possible.

The man stands there as the patch grows bigger. He looks stunned. Like he doesn't believe something. Like on telly when they've just been shot. Slowly he turns, staggers out the door.

I look up at Mr Canning. He has forgotten about me.

"Did you not see? Did you not see? That man weed in his pants," you say.

Mr Canning sighs. "Are you still here?" he says grumpily. "Why don't you go home? Always under my feet."

You don't move, stay staring up at him.

"Will you show me the shotgun?" you ask.

He looks at you. His eyes are tired. He speaks wearily, "Go

home lad and play with your toys while you still can. Your questions will be the death of me."

"Did you hear about the dirty egg," you say, "it went around with its yoke hanging out."

Mr Canning opens the door and points out. You trail through it despondently. Home to the shadows. You forgot to show him the conker.

Later you say to your mother that you would like to have a watch with a second hand. She doesn't hear you. She is very distracted these days. The face in the wallpaper laughs at you that night. "It's your fault," it says. "What's my fault?" you say. "Everything," it says. The sandstorm comes early. You stay under the blankets until you begin to sweat. You put your head out. The face in the wallpaper is asleep. The sandstorm is gone. You think of the skylight. Tomorrow you have a day off school. You sleep.

You are woken early by soft licks of his brush. It is the man who sweeps the streets. Each day he brushes away the darkness letting the morning light in. If you look out he is a matchstick silhouette against the inky morning with his long hinged arms that end in yard brush and shovel. He moves these wooden limbs with a soft deft skill pulling the sleepy residue of the streets into the width of his shovel palm. Then with a rattle, everything is thrown into his little trolley bin. On he creaks, the street a tinge brighter in his trail. You wonder what time is it. Everything now lies strange and vulnerable. The houses stand shivering and bleary-eyed. The windows blink open as occasional lights shine through netted curtains. A car drifts by, its engine giving a throaty morning cough. A bike clips along the road, its trim wheels braking, then with a slow yawn speeding up again as the slight hill takes it. A brisk walker prompts you with his clipped organised bank official walk. Then silence falls again except for the soft whispers of the yard brush. Wake up it says. Wake up. Wake up. The face in the wallpaper hides in the dim light of the room. It cannot yet be seen but he is there. You get up before he wakes.

This morning nobody pays you any attention. The face in the wallpaper follows you from room to room. "In the wa-ay. In the wa-ay," it chants. You leave the house for the brightness of the street. You lean against the wall and shoot passers-by through your fingers. Mr Kelly across the street takes one to the chest and drops like a ton of bricks. You sharpen a lollipop stick. You look for something to stab. Nothing. No one.

The American is still closed. The navy blinds block the windows. Sulkily you push at the door. To your surprise it opens. You stick your head inside. It is dark. There is a strange hush. You let yourself in and the street recedes into the background. It feels cold in here. There is no comfortable glow of heat and company. To your horror you discover that shadows live in here also, cultivated by the darkness and the silence. The toilets hiss and throw out their bitter, pissy smell. The fox looks down. Its brown stained teeth open in a grin. "Hello," it says, "what do we have here? A juicy, tasty little boy. Mmmmm."

Its legs tense. Is it going to jump at you? You glance at the mirror. It points into the scullery. Mr Canning uses it to look out on the pub when he has to do work there. The back of his head appears. "Surprise," you want to say, like in the comics. But something makes you stop. "Shhhs," says the fox, "watch this. It's quite a show."

Mr Canning's head is slightly bent. He bends down further and picks something up. You recognise the barrel of the shotgun. You nearly laugh in glee. Maybe now he'll let you touch the gun. But you stay silent. A shiver travels down your back. The fox pins you with his sly, green eye. "Do you know what's happening? Do you know what's happening. Go ask the face in the wallpaper it will tell you what's happening. It knows everything." You are breathing heavily. You glance back. Mr Canning has placed the gun in his mouth. His head is moving slightly. A tension grips you. What is happening? The postcards glow an eerie blue. His shoulders tilt. A muscle pulls in his neck. Your breathing is harsh. You want to run.

You turn. Your heel grinds on the stone floor. A tic movement in his head. Suddenly the Angelus bells ring out. Ding. Ding. Ding. You are gone. The sudden brightness of the street consumes you. Cars speed by. You run to the river. You look for sprats. You stay there for a while. On the way home you see Mr Canning staring out the window of the bar. He looks at you for a second and then looks away.

Later that day your mother takes you to Cronin's and buys you a watch. You have been a very good boy. You look at the watch trying to see the actual movement of the hands. You place it to your ear. You delight in its tick. Time has a meaning now. Every second that goes by means that you are a second older. The face in the wallpaper clicks its teeth. "You've a watch. Getting tall. You better cop on quick to what's going on. What was Mr Canning doing? Do you know? Ah you know nothing. But I can tell you. Do you want to hear? Do you want to hear?" You ignore it. You are too happy with your watch. Another time. You go into the American and show it to Mr Canning. He peers down at it. "God I thought there were enough clocks and watches in the world," he says. It's a funny comment. He gives you a packet of crisps. Your new watch tells you it's only six o'clock. You have time to go to the river and try and catch sprats. Someday you will catch a fish.

Maureen Aitken

Winner of the 1999 Fish Short Story Prize

When I was little my family (two parents and two siblings) took the front parts of the station wagon on vacations, but I got the back: huddled between suitcases, watching the hills shrink. On one of the drives my family started to scream, and I didn't see until after how the road plunged and at the bottom construction workers had cracked a huge hole into the street. Someone yelled stop, so my father sped up, and the mammoth orange station wagon lifted off the road and landed with a thud on the other side of the ditch. There I saw the construction workers, clapping mightily, cheering, giving the thumbs up, and rushing to put up the barricades before any more people like us, the risky and the sometimes lucky, took one too many chances. Wow, I thought, this is living. I learned later that this sort of moment, snagged between fear and amazement, is storytelling, too.

This is Art

Maureen Aitken

In August, when the cicadas burned and the lawnmowers sounded like industrial bees, we couldn't stop. In the bedroom, on the couch, on the floor, and afterwards we would lie there, reading the paper, or letting the television taunt us like a car salesman. Jack would wiggle his toes against mine, and we'd look at one another for a long time. His face was like a catcher's mitt, warm and beaten. He reminded me of the boys who had moved away when I was little, but now he was a man. Then it would start all over again and I felt like one of those cicadas burning up from something that had no name. The dog licked our legs. The mail fell through the slot. But we wouldn't move. Even a smile felt like it would slice through us.

I didn't know if we were fragile or potent or both, but one conversation dangled on us like an ornament. On a rainy and bruised July day, he had turned to me, with his sturdy face and said, "In September, when the summer's gone, you'll change your mind."

"That's crazy," I said.

He didn't look afraid or worried or any of those emotions that could be clicked back into joint.

"I just know," and he put his palm on my arm and I thought it would sear through me.

We weren't crazy at first, we met at the institute where he had been farmed out by his company to do some on-site design. I knew from the start he was one of these people who wouldn't stay long. He wore New Balance tennis shoes and a T-shirt. He was tall and 30, and he used to throw paper airplanes on my desk, and the picture of his big fists folding the paper carefully, adjusting the nose point broke my heart a little. He wrote notes inside the airplanes, "You work too hard" and "Your boss is sort of a dink." He took nothing seriously, which meant the secretaries appreciated him, one after another of the art staff said, "So, do you paint?"

He thought they were all obnoxious, and told me so on the first date. We went to art movies – Jarmush, and Fellini – and it's true when I looked at the screen, I could see him there, riding through on the mystery train.

Nothing really happened on the first three dates. On the fourth we sat at tables and drank fishbowl margaritas and talked about how Bruno, my boss, walked tight. We mocked him, picking up salt shakers, and forks and pennies off the table and saying, "Now this is art." And under the table, all the while, I pressed my heel into my leg, and thought this is what it feels like, if you fall for someone enigmatic, this is what you get.

So he just wanted to be friends, I thought. Friends are good. And a friend who can lift things. I don't have one of those. As soon as I thought that, he leaned over and kissed me. We were at a table outside, with our finished margaritas licked clean of the salt, and I felt as though something enormous had just swept through town. Time's rigor seemed to lift itself up, like a needle off an old record. It was June.

On Monday mornings we left the couch and the floor, and the dog with that tilted, where do you go? look. I drove to my job at the institute, and Jack went back downtown, to the main computer graphics shop where he would be shipped out again in a week or two. Most days he would call and say things like, I cleaned all the spots off the Blazers or I'm creating mountains. It's perfect, it's all perfect. He seemed to forget about our impending finale, and I didn't remind him. In my most hopeful moments, I thought of September, when the leaves began to show off, and when I'd be able to say, "Ha, you were wrong."

Bruno had a laundry list of duties. Prep the slides for the next exhibit on Kandinsky, and run through the October exhibit with the theme, 'Love in Dangerous Times.'

My job was called assistant to the curator, and mostly it meant driving around in his Benz, and answering his car phone. "Oh, Susan, could you swing by the Fisch gallery and pick up a package waiting for us?" and "Sue, could you run out to the library and pick up some articles on Liechtenstein? We need them for the blurb."

While every moment proved Jack's point about Bruno, I loved being outside, and the smell of the leather seats, and I used to drive down the street where a couple of painters lived just so they could point and laugh and flip me the bird.

I had lost sight of that street's face years ago, and believed it was beautiful. In the Benz, I was reminded of the exhausted roofs and the rusty metal porch chairs. It was like someone telling you your mother was ugly, and for one frightening second you saw through their eyes. But I still liked the joke of rolling up in the Benz, and sometimes Jan and Carl would walk downstairs and if they didn't have any paint on them we'd drive around, or maybe I'd drop them downtown, and on the way they'd say, "So when are you going to put one of my paintings in your swanky institute?"

One time Jan said, "Take us to a fancy spot" and I drove and drove, past the apartments, and the little bars, and the big-business buildings where you couldn't park for all the people. Finally, I drove them to the Whitney, a brownstone restaurant with white lights like stars, even in the day. The valet came up and tried to open the door, and I hit the button so the window lowered and said, "Can we just sit here?"

"Hey blood," the valet said, "that you, man?" and Carl said, yeah. They swept hands and nodded and the valet said, "You're rolling now," and he kept nodding even as he held up his two fingers and mouthed the word peace just before a BMW drove up and the valet sank into himself. We could see his face stiffen. His hand move out gently to open the car door, and he said "good afternoon." We sat for a minute and a quietness fell over us, and it wasn't a joke anymore. Jan said, "We'll walk home," and Carl said, "Yeah, good idea. Don't forget about the institute, Sue," he said, pounding his chest. "Get me while I'm cheap, man."

Sometimes I would just drive around alone and think about Jack. If he only knew how the prediction didn't fit my life. Most of the time I was the one who couldn't let go. But pound for pound when the heartache eased, like the swell off a sprain, I'd get a phone call from the ex. I'd joke, just to ease the sting. One time I said:

"Hey Jim, my ex, are you excellent, excited, exceptional today?"

A long pause followed, then a regretful sigh and I thought uh oh.

"Can we talk?" Jim said.

Though my temptation was to put that phone down and run to a very long movie, I said, "Sure." Jim said, "I really miss you," in a way that surprised himself.

"No, you don't, you don't want me," I said. "You weren't happy."

"No," he said, "I was fucked up I was." And I'd have to run down the litany of bummers, like the beads on a rosary that I had told myself over and over again to ease the pain long ago. On the phone I said it again to keep everything from ripping back open.

"I didn't like your friends, I didn't waterski, I didn't know what to say to any of the other women at the parties," I said. "I was always making you leave early. Remember when I made frown faces with the sushi?"

"They're just parties," he said, "I'm sure now, I'm so sure," and he kept trying to convince me until I blurted out what I didn't even know was true until that moment. "It's over."

After saying goodbye, I turned off the ringer and shoved two pillows over my head and hoped to God he didn't realize too late what he had thrown away.

Bruno called me on the car phone and said, "Sue, could you pick up some food, anyplace, I'm starving without the car. You know what I like, no fast food."

"Sure," I said, and I hung up the phone, and looked down the street, and all I saw were McDonald's and Burger King, and Kentucky Fried Chicken, Popeye's. And in the distance they look almost like telephone poles, or stop signs, that repeated and repeated at just the same stride until the eye could not know to see them anymore. What a weird knowledge, to understand that their order carried out beyond my view, across the country. For every three miles a McDonald's, and for every exit, an order. To think of it wore me out: the way the view went on that way across the country, out past my wildest imagination.

After work I took my shower and sat on Jack's wood porch cleaning corn. I wore a violet dress my mother had given me, and if a couple of holes seemed unfashionable, it was tender. I felt the wood on my feet and the day bled out of me. Jack came home with his sunglasses half down his nose and put his palm on my arm and walked upstairs to take his shower. Sometimes I felt as though we were living two lives – the work life of coffee in white mugs and central air, and here with open windows and floors worn with our paths.

Jack came out and put his arm around me and said, "Steak?" and I said, "Chicken," and his face fell a little and when I added, "Barbecue," he brightened. We sat without saying much. I wanted to ask him. But if he said it again, I thought we would break. This can't be good, I thought, that one sentence could crush us.

The dog whined to be let out. I looked at Jack, and somehow that warning July voice and his face linked up, like charms on a heavy bracelet. After dinner we sat on the porch and he said,

"Today I took the glare off a few cars, and then I made a moon. They don't want Blazers on mountain tops. They want them on the moon, now. The earth isn't good enough anymore."

I stared ahead at a neighbor, Betty, in the garden and Mr Johnson mending his fence. I said, "You're bitter."

I had never criticized him before, and he turned and looked at me.

"Bitter?" he said. He looked down the road that dead-ended. "Compared to who?"

"You complain about this job and you stay there," I said. "If you hate it, fix it."

I couldn't help it. What he had said in July grew like some phantom pregnancy. Sometimes at night when he was asleep I would stare at his open mouth and think, he believes we will end. And saying it would end made me feel a loss coming on, and I wanted him more. I wanted the weekends all the time.

When it got dark, he turned sullen. We lay on the couch watching sitcoms that weren't funny, and he kissed the back of my shoulder in a steady, distant manner that let me know he was thinking. In the morning, the dog watched us go with his curious expression and we held hands out to our cars.

"Have a good day," I said.

"Yeah."

We kissed and we walked apart. It took forever for our fingers to separate. As I drove in, the road looked cold, and I couldn't find a free parking space, so I gave the attendant my $5. I don't know why I drove. It was just half a mile, but every inch depressed me. I looked at the white stone institute with the purple film society sign and a Cadillac parked in front. Bruno didn't have any errands for me. All day we organized slides of the exhibit. We moved Lange's 'Migrant Mother' next to 'Lucretia' but then shifted her near 'The Order of Angels". The Founder's Society planned a fundraising party for the opening night of the exhibit. I couldn't call the artists directly, I had to call their people, and tried to find one who would fly out for the night.

Finally Bruno ran his eye over all the pieces again and shook his head. We walked through the gallery, and I wrote down the positions in my pad.

"It's not right," he said. He tapped his foot. "Something – I just don't know."

Bruno folded his arms and sulked right up until I left for the day. I walked outside with the bright sun, and the air so hot and polluted it ate through me. The steering wheel hurt, and I lifted up my skirt and draped the hem over the black plastic and made my way home.

The light turned red. The light turned green, and I thought, oh God, what have I done?

I took my shower and waited on the piece of the porch where the shade hung low. I couldn't stop worrying that I had ruined it, out of fear or spite for believing we would end. When Jack came home, I said, I'm sorry.

He kissed me on the cheek and said, I'll be down. He took his shower and found me on the porch with my arms around my knees.

He gave me a beer, and clinked his to mine.

"Congratulate me," he said, "I quit."

The beer tasted icy and I leaned against his shoulder.

"I thought I could keep a perspective but you buy into it anyway, through the resentment," he said. "You were wrong, but you were right."

He looked out and drank.

"Jack, are we falling apart, or what?" I said.

"Huh?"

"You said we were going to fall apart in September," I said. "Jesus, if you're going to send me into a tailspin, at least have the good grace to remember."

"I forgot that a long time ago."

He didn't look at me.

"Liar," I said.

"It was nothing, a nightmare, or being pissed about something."

"Why would you say it if you didn't mean it?"

"Look, it's different now."

"Different how?" I asked.

He took my hand and said, "This is the part where things get complicated. This is the part where I leave."

"I don't get it," I said, and my heart was sinking.

"Before, you know. I'd cut out now. I'm tired of leaving. Now I want something else, you, and something else."

"What?" I asked.

I feared the way his eyes fell to the lawn and the way he stared there for a minute. A minute turned into two. I put my arm around him and he grabbed me hard, and I wished I could open that locked door of him, but the key was somewhere in other women who had left him and been left, somewhere in his mother's voice, in his friends joking in the middle of the night. Maybe the answers came from something else, something so big he didn't know how to look at it anymore. Or maybe this was all a con, and he'd be gone tomorrow.

The next two weeks Jack drove around a lot. Sometimes we'd drive together, and I'd point to buildings with American flags in the windows, and Coke bottles with candles, and say, I lived there.

We drove to his old place, and it was rotten, boarded up and spray painted. Grass grew high. Jack said he'd been robbed there so many times, he'd lost count.

"I moved in with everything, the guitar, the television, the goldfish. I left with a can of chili."

At home one night I said, "Maybe you could work with me? They liked you."

"Don't nag me woman."

"Oh yeah?" I pounded a pillow into his face and said, "Here's to your computerized sunset, Jack," and he took the heavier seat cushion and said, "Here's to your art farts," and we went at it until the dog came up and barked as if to say, Fun. You're having fun. And then we smacked him too and the dog barked more and his tail wagged. He tore a hole in the seat cushion and tried to lick the stuffing.

At the end of the two weeks, Jack came home and didn't take a shower. My hair was still wet, and he went inside and grabbed my shoes.

"Come on," he said.

We drove past our couple of blocks and by the old record studio, where Aretha Franklin and The Temptations recorded three decades ago. We stopped. The car smelled like sweat and newspapers, and I wanted out. He opened the door and said, come on. He put his hands over my eyes and walked me up to the corner. I didn't trust the ground. I walked with high lifted steps and thought there is a curb here, somewhere there is a curb.

"You excited?"

"No," I said. "But I'm afraid."

He pulled his palm away.

"Look," he said.

The one-story red-brick building hid behind a thick matte of weeds and grass. A screen door hung on half a hinge, and a yellowed, ripped shade drooped in the window. More than one drunk had used the space as a dumping ground for liquor bottles. The fence had been peeled back, and on one of the prongs, a pair of men's jockeys hung like a flag.

"Yeah," I said. "And?"

"It's selling for a $1," Jack said.

Something moved in the weeds and I stepped back.

"Hold out, Jack," I said. "You could get it for 50 cents."

His mouth was right next to my ear. His arms were around my stomach.

"Too late," he said. "I'm going to make it good."

I knew he had saved money. He was so happy. Happier than I'd seen him in a long time.

"Great," I said. "That's great."

And I knew what my mother felt like the day I came home with my hair dyed blue.

Bruno and I worked late the next couple of nights to organize the show. It took four days to find a good painter who would fly out and lecture on the show. Bruno settled on an arrangement. It was seven when we looked over all the slides, and finally, he grabbed my arm, and seethed, "We've done it. This is a triumph."

I smiled. It was one of those strange moments that made up for all Bruno's snobbery and his tight walk. He sat back, pulled a bottle of Scotch from the drawer, and poured us both one.

"Fine work," he said to me. "Jesus I'm great."

We swallowed the shots. I walked outside. Though the air was hot it had already broken a little. I could smell the moss starting in the leaves. As I drove by the huge museum, I knew Bruno was right. It was art. But now the museum was closed. A driver in a Fairmont passed. His bumper had fallen off. The pipe scraped. And where I waited, all I could see were more of the same: McDonald's, Burger King. I wanted to hit something.

I stopped at Jack's little place. A windowless storage building overshadowed Jack's hope like a bully, and not much else on the block survived. Three houses across the street slumped in the evening sun. They were the sort of homes that had belonged to a family once. But that was a long time ago, and newer owners converted the homes into apartments. Around them empty lots, and at the corner, a building with grates on the windows and a 'For Lease' sign painted by hand. I looked back at the place and my face reflected in the window. It was a face I recognized, but in my heart, did not want to know. This face said, expect the worst. I turned away and looked back again. I remembered thinking this when I was young. In high school, some friend cried about failing a test. We smoked cigarettes and I rolled the burning end on the step so the ashes flaked off. I said: you hoped too much. Expect the worst, then you won't be disappointed. Then you won't get hurt. "You're right," she had said. "I won't let them get to me again. Fuck 'em."

I don't know where I got such an idea. But I could feel it in the job, and in the apartments with the Coke bottle candles. In this face reflecting off of Jack's ambitions.

Maybe I got it from my parents, or their parents, or maybe this is all my own invention. But when I looked around, I could see by the way the view piled up. This tough talk, these safe bets were growing in the weeds, and in the houses. In the McDonald's, and in the buildings left behind. It was in the history, and in the junk: expect the worst. And when you expect the worst, you settle for boarded buildings, you give in to the anger, you give in to the bitterness, you give in.

Buttercups grew in the weeds, and I pulled a few. The moon was early, and hung in the daytime sky like a wafer. I walked out to the car, and looked back at the building. The windows still looked lonely, and I thought the place needed a light in the window, or a car parked out front. So I left the car there and walked home. I know it sounds funny, but when I glanced back, the place looked a little more like someone lived there, like it belonged.

As I walked, past the parking lot of the old record studio, and towards home, that's when I felt this warmth, this energy rumbling through me so hard, I knew something big was going to change. Or maybe it already had. I could only see this road, and the crumbling building, and those horrible things that stayed the same. And I thought we could pull Jan and Carl into it. They'd sneer at first about it all being beneath them. But after the bitching, they'd pat my back, and say, cool, and Carl would put up his fist and say, we're in.

I walked by a newspaper box. Because of work I'd missed everything. There were strikes, and fires. Shootings. Much was the same. I looked for the weather, sunny and hot tomorrow, and the date caught me. September 1.

137

I ran home. Jack had showered, and sat on the porch with the dog. The sunset was on him like a fire. The dog barked and ran to me, and Jack stood up and started to walk, with the fire on him, and his hair like gold. I would change my mind: I thought that was what he had said. And in that moment, I couldn't say he was wrong. Everything had changed. The summer was giving in. The flower petals browned at the tips. I thought for the first time people come into your life at just the right moment. What can you do but try? And he walked to me, and I thought I hadn't been this happy and lonely in a long long time. Maybe never before. It was Friday night, and we had the whole weekend, and believing in the worst seemed like the most ridiculous thing imaginable. Someone else could have the sameness that was out there, down a road and out past the suburbs, out beyond my belief. Nothing good is a line. What was beautiful knew how to veer on a whim. We trust the ground, but dream in motion. What I wanted traveled within us and without a name, like a car plunging into the darkness, like some roadside travel agent yelling screw the maps. Learn the road, baby, and you'll find your way.

Mick Wood

Winner of the 1999 Fish Short Story Prize

Born and raised in commuter-belt Essex, the young Mick — inspired by the likes of fellow Basildon electro-boppers Depeche Mode — dreamt only of pop stardom. Several years, in the late 70s / early 80s, spent fronting various obscure bands that were every bit as pretentious and doomed as Mysterical cured him of that. There followed stints as a builders' merchant, art student and photographer before he gained a degree in Theatre Studies from Lancaster University. In 1990 he moved to Leeds and became a founder member of Interference Theatre. Mick was a winner of the 1997 Ian St James Awards and has written extensively for small-scale theatre and cabaret.

Heard of a Band Called Mysterical?

Mick Wood

The black-and-white footage is fashionably unsteady, the camera jerking wildly from side to side as, at a trot, it follows Mysterical out of Emma's basement flat and up the crumbling steps. Some years later (but not *too* many) as a moment in an MTV retrospective, and by way of poignant contrast, the ascent of these grotty steps is cut with shots of them mounting the stage in a vast stadium. The crowd roars, thousands of flashlights burst around them, a famous American actor stridently heralds their arrival over the P.A. . . . But for now the film-makers, also yet to be discovered, tag along as these elegant, decadent imps skip up the deserted, windswept high street. High as kites, the band make faces at the camera, toss clever quips and puns to the film crew. These witticisms become folklore for their fans – 'I love that bit when Paul says Emma is "the voice of reason" and Jimmy says "more like the *void* of reason".'

To Jimmy this is how it was. These were "the early days", moments in a fly-on-the-wall documentary that would lie undiscovered for years in the back of a junk shop.

But there were no cameras, and none of them were high on anything, or even drunk, since their finances had only stretched to a few bottles of cheap Belgian lager. And you could hardly describe any of them as impish, even Jimmy, who was trying so hard. Despite his constant prompting the others refused to behave in a manner consistent with Jimmy's fantasy, pursuing the night's activities instead with an embarrassment and business-like gravity that he found baffling and increasingly irritating.

They were having trouble getting started. 'What about here?' Jimmy said, trying out one of his mischievous faces in the window of The Olive Tree Cafe.

Which was ironic, since it was at The Olive Tree that they met on Saturday afternoons to laugh at the passers-by who stole sly glances at themselves in that most reflective of windows. Emma especially enjoyed this. She called the window her "two-way mirror", and was convinced that the phenomenon had some bearing on "the human condition".

'The men are the worst, have you noticed that, how vain the men are?'

She wrote some lyrics about it:

'Sitting here with the world passing by
Got to leave this place and find the reason why
Why I'm always on the outside looking in
Why I can't tell the sinner from the sin

Two-way mirror, yeah
Life's just a two-way mirror
A two-way mirror for me and you.'

She called it 'Two-Way Mirror'.

Paul liked the title, but didn't much care for the content. It made no sense to him, and, on reflection, she was inclined to agree.

'I just wrote down what came into my head.'

'You see, you can't do that with lyrics. They're like poetry, you've got to work and work at them, it takes a lot of effort to make it look effortless. Sometimes I spend an entire day on one line.'

More of Paul's poetry later. Suffice to say, for now, that he wrote the lyrics to all their songs.

'No, it's not right, it's no good here, it'd be a waste.'

Paul and Jimmy were arguing now.

'Fucking hell Paul, I thought you said we should blitz it, isn't that what he said? We should put them everywhere? We've come a mile and we haven't put one up yet.'

'They'd be no good up this end of town, no one would look at them.'

'Oh no, then why have Red Monkey put all those posters over there?'

'They're ten feet fucking high.'

'So?'

'So we couldn't compete with that.'

Tzannis and Emma leant against the window of the cafe and waited – Tzannis for an appropriate moment to intervene, Emma for Tzannis to exercise his usual diplomacy. She didn't have to wait too long.

'Paul's right, we couldn't have put any up so far. But I think Jimmy's got a point, I'll ask dad to put a couple in the window.'

'Oh Tzannis, Tzannis,' thought Emma, 'get off that bloody fence.'

Tzannis' family ran The Olive Tree. It was there that he had been asked to join the band, after the others, during one of their Saturday sessions, heard him practising in a storeroom at the back. His father, a large, jovial man, had drawn their attention to it, performing a peculiar shuffling dance to the complex bass lines as he worked behind the counter. He was proud of his boy, with good cause.

'All right Tzannis, fine,' said Paul, 'but you have to tell him – if anyone asks he mustn't say that it's his son's band, he has to say he doesn't know who we are. He mustn't say he knows us.'

'Whatever.'

'Now then,' said Emma, 'do you think we could get on with it?'

'The voice of reason,' said Paul, smiling ingratiatingly at her.

Which prompted Jimmy's legendary response.

A stretch of temporary fencing opposite the cinema was the place they first settled on – so temporary, in fact, that it was taken down the very next day, broken up and disposed of in a nearby skip, a few of their torn posters remaining just visible amongst the rubble.

They had just got started when they found themselves captured in a pair of ominously slowing headlights. Mysterical, mid-paste, froze in a tableau that they would have captioned "Counter Revolutionaries Caught in an Act of Subversion by the Secret Police", but would have been more appropriately entitled "Local Sixth Formers in Contemporary Dance/Mime Workshop".

An electric window glided down with the faintest purr. A hand, the stubby fingers thick with sovereign rings, emerged from the darkness within and grasped the top of the door.

'All right guys, what you doin'?'

A mouth became visible, chewing as it spoke. Paul broke out of the tableau and shuffled a little nearer to the car, limp, dripping paste brush dangling from his hand.

'Putting up some posters,' he said, far more sheepishly than he would have wished.

'Right, yeah, listen, know this area do you, yeah?' A head was suddenly thrust from the window – the roundest and whitest head that they had ever seen. There appeared to be no neck, the head balancing directly, precariously on a red collar and gold satin tie. A widow's peak of cropped black hair formed a high arching M over the smooth forehead. The eyes were small black buttons, like a puppet's eyes, and the tiny ears stuck out like pale, crumpled fungi. The lipless mouth ground on tirelessly. Occasionally they caught sight of the unfortunate piece of gum, haplessly tossed in a pink maw.

Paul was relieved and ashamed to see Tzannis step confidently up to the window.

'Where are you looking for?'

144

'Oh, er, where was it again?'

From the passenger side came a very deep voice.

'Lister Road.'

The round head bobbled about appropriately as Tzannis gave the directions, but it didn't appear to be really listening. Those vacant black buttons seemed almost to be counting the members of Mysterical, making a meticulous note of their attire, the way they were standing, the expressions on their faces. They felt as if they were being scanned by an android.

'Yeah, great, cheers. Listen, I've er, just been doing some deliveries 'round here and I've got a bit of surplus stock, watches, jewellery and that, yeah? I don't know if you fancy having a look?'

Tzannis declined the kind offer on their behalf.

'Fine, no problem. What's that you got there then?'

To Paul's further dismay Jimmy, unrolling a poster, moved to the car.

'They're posters, for our band.'

The poster was black with a thin white border made up of row upon row of tiny question marks. There was no other design or picture on it, just the following, in bold lettering and an unusual, elongated font that Paul had found on his fathers PC: "HEARD OF A BAND CALLED MYSTERICAL?"

Paul's idea. Paul's design. The backbone of Paul's ingenious plan.

He had put it to them in The Olive Tree one Saturday: two rounds of postering. The first batch of posters to convey purely the enigmatic question above, the second, placed two or three weeks later, to give details of their first gig.

'It's a technique they use all the time in advertising.'

'I don't know that I'd be very comfortable with that, using marketing tricks. Marketing, it's just another word for lying as far as I'm concerned.'

'Nothing wrong with it Emma, as long as the product isn't shit. I agree with you, if the product's shit, but we know ours isn't.'

145

'Our music isn't a "product".'

'No, no, of course not, but you know what I mean. What we've got to do is get a following, create a bit of a buzz.'

'A "buzz"? Oh please!' Donald had sipped languidly at an espresso and pushed a heavy, stray lock of hair from his angular cheek.

Donald Bliss. How they had laughed at that name when, after placing an advert for a keyboard player in the *Melody Maker*, his letter had arrived. 'A nineteenth-century composer of organ music,' imagined Emma. 'A wanker,' imagined Jimmy, and got a bigger laugh. Tzannis had suggested they look at him anyway since he had grade five piano. 'Grade five piano?' scoffed Paul, 'what the fuck?'

By the time they were plotting their imminent and sudden rise to cult status, the svelte, elfin, beautiful Donald was very much a part of the team.

Contemplating Paul's proposal, Donald had stretched his long legs out under the table and lay back in his seat, noting the satisfying way his jeans formed a sizeable pouch around his genitals. Under the table his electric foot had touched Emma's leg, causing her to recoil instantly and violently.

'Well it might work, but you'd . . .' – when referring to the band Donald always said 'you'd' rather than 'we'd' – '. . . you'd have to really blitz the streets.'

On the night in question Donald came down with the most debilitating headache and, regretfully, had to stay at home. Emma suggested to the others that, if they happened to pass his flat, they should drop in and see if he needed anything. She knew how awful it was to be ill and on your own.

'Yeah, wicked, got any gigs?'

It turned out that the round-faced man was well connected in the local music scene and had managed quite a few local bands in their early days, some of whom had gone on to great things. He

146

produced from the glove compartment an early CD of a band called Best Defense – a favourite of Paul's – cut when they were still on a small, independent label. Sure enough, there on the credits was a reference to their manager, Darren Hitching.

'That's me. Dropped me like a hot potato when they got taken up. Still, I'm not bitter. I'll have to come along to your gig. I know a few people, might be able to get you a few dates, if you're any good. Nothing big, just local stuff, but it's a start innit.'

Paul, seeing the man in the car in an entirely new light, thought it best if he handled this, the business end of things. Clearing the others out of the way he provided Mr Hitching with the date of their first gig and details as to how he could obtain a complimentary ticket. He also gave him his home phone number – a decision he would come to rue in the months ahead.

'Just one thing,' said Darren, waving Paul nearer so that the others couldn't hear. 'If I was you, I'd lose the Greek. You know what's going to happen don't you? He's going to bring his parents along to the first gig, maybe the whole family. Hasn't he hinted as much? That dad of his, he's going to show you all up by doing some Greek dance right in front of the stage, you'll look out and there he'll be, arms above his head, stamping and shaking his shoulders, everyone looking at him. And it's not just that. He's got some funny ideas about music. These trained musicians, they might be able to play their instruments but they've got no creativity. You know what I'm saying? Their minds are too structured, they're too caught up in keys and bars and sharps and flats. Whereas you, people like you, you just know what *sounds good*. Its something natural, a gift. And I don't want to get personal but, well, look at him. You've got to think of your image. Image is everything in this game. You take my advice. Lose the Greek.'

Paul turned to look at Tzannis, who was now some way off, examining a likely lamp post with the others. It was the only street lamp working at that end of the street, and the three of them were floating on a disc of orange light in a black void.

When Paul turned back the car had moved away.

Emma put a hand on his shoulder.

'Are you all right?'

'You see,' he said, 'we're making contacts already.'

'Those kind of contacts we can do without,' said Tzannis, taking the brush from him and starting to paste.

To Jimmy the encounter was already in print. Page one chapter one of the official biography. 'Some bands, they spend years paying their dues, but Mysterical seemed to get the breaks, right from the start. Take that chilly September night . . .'

Paul, too, felt a sense of destiny.

Donald was standing by the window having a post-coital joint when the rest of Mysterical swept around the corner of the street below, looking, with their long coats and wild hair, like an obscure sect of medieval penitents, a fat confessor in the shape of Tzannis leading the way. A naked young girl lay on her front on the bed behind him, kicking her feet above her boyish buttocks. Donald wouldn't normally have minded being seen naked at the window, his pendulous, barely flaccid cock silhouetted against the light in the room, but he ducked back behind the curtain now.

'Bloody hell, it's the band. Look, I don't suppose you'd do me a favour?'

The girl, dressed in one of Donald's jumpers and nothing more, opened the door on a briefly grinning Emma, who only completed half a sentence.

'We found ourselves on this side of town and we just thought we'd . . .'

The girl invited them in for coffee, telling them that Donald's head was so bad that he'd had to go to bed – which is where he should have been anyway, since it was one o'clock in the morning. Jimmy went with her to the kitchen to help with the cups.

To Jimmy, who could smell the pungent, alluring aroma of sex on her, this girl was truly decadent. He saw her in a grainy black-and-white photograph, propped up in a huge bed in a hotel somewhere, joint in one hand and bottle of vodka in the other, flanked by him and Donald.

Life on the road.

As she made the coffee, dancing around the kitchen on her tiny, delicate bare feet, the girl sang a song. Jimmy was entranced. She had the voice of an angel – fey, slightly clipped, a charming little chirrup at the end of the lines:

'Cold comfort in a warm climate
Warm feelings for a cold heart.'

'Who's that by?' he asked.

'It's something I wrote myself, it's a bit of a hobby of mine.'

'Sounds good.'

'No, not really. A friend of mine at art school, her cousin knows Ross out of Tarr – she said I should send him a demo.'

'You should.'

'Oh, I don't know.'

She sang some more as she poured the water into the cups, the same two lines several times over. Each repetition was an ingenious variation of rhythm and melody. She might suddenly plunge down to a deep velvety note then slide, oh so gently, up again, quivering with vibrato, the notes rising and fading like lark song, so high and pure that Jimmy thought his heart would break with the beauty of it. So transcendentally sweet was the tune and its variations that it had a peculiar effect on Jimmy. Light-headed, dizzy, he felt his feet lifting from the floor. Curling over and tucking up his knees he allowed himself to drift up to the ceiling.

The light fitting bumped gently at his back. The girl, holding two cups of coffee, looked up at him. She managed to keep singing as she spoke.

'Donald has told me all about your band. Do you mind if I speak frankly? If I was you I'd lose that girl. She can sing, but her voice is so undistinctive. There's more to singing in a band than just being able to hold a tune. And, well, she doesn't exactly look right, does she? You know what she'll be like on tour. She won't want to take any drugs and she'll insist on getting early nights. There'll be no trashing of hotel rooms when she's about. It's so important to have the right person fronting a band, that's what my friend's cousin's friend says. You have to have someone with a bit of charisma, someone enigmatic, someone with presence. All bands have their early casualties. It'll be in the first chapter of the autobiography, how you had to make the difficult but essential decision to lose that girl.'

She handed Jimmy a cup of coffee, but he took it by the body of the cup, which was scalding hot, and had to drop it.

'Damn, sorry.'

'No, it's all right. Your poor hand.'

Taking him by the wrist she kissed him gently on the palm.

In the sitting room an animated Tzannis was discussing an idea he'd had.

'In 'Casualty', you know where it goes down after the second verse? I reckon we should change key for the middle eight, make it darker, I could play dmm, dmm dmm da, da, dmm dmm.'

Paul was looking at Emma and laughing. 'Change key? Middle eight? What the fuck is he talking about?'

The posters weren't going to stretch as far as they thought. Up to now they had been putting them up in clusters of four or six, partly to cover larger posters that were already there – they had only been able to afford A4 – and partly to create impact. Now there was a heated debate on the wisdom of this. Jimmy and Emma revealed that they had thought it a mistake to put them up like that in the first place.

'It looks desperate, too pushy, like we don't have confidence in just the one.'

Paul was seething. He questioned, not for the first time, why they always left him to make all the decisions then complained about it afterwards.

The burdens of leadership.

Tzannis' contribution to the debate was fairly typical.

'Ideally I think that Paul's right, but seeing as we're running a bit low I think perhaps that from now on we should just stick to the single poster option.'

They glared at him.

As they mounted the stopped escalator that connected the main square with the St. George shopping precinct the bickering bubbled on.

'Anyway, it was Donald who suggested we "blitz it",' said Paul, much to Emma's disgust, 'I was all for restraint, right from the start, if you remember.'

The sudden approach of a towering figure in a peaked cap and dark suit cut the argument short. To Emma it seemed as if he had stepped out of the wall.

'I hope you're not going to put any of those up here,' he said, pointing a torch at the posters.

Tzannis assured him that they weren't.

'Let's have a look then.' The peak of the cap cast a deep shadow over the top half of his face. Just visible were two red glints where a light from the square below was reflected in his eyes. The movement of the mouth was lost in a thick black beard which covered the entire visible area of his face. 'Come on, I'm not going to shop you. I was once in the business myself, believe it or not.'

Jimmy unrolled a poster.

'No, quite right, I haven't ever heard of them. That's you lot is it?'

They nodded guiltily, as if expecting a cuff 'round the ear – except, that is, for Tzannis, who turned away and looked out over the railing.

'Have you ever heard of a band called The Shoemakers?'

They hadn't.

'No? Well, your parents will have. You ask them about The Shoemakers. Number three we got to in 1968 with *Run Baby Run*.'

A disturbing sound emerged from the beard. An incantation, very flat, very deep and phlegmy. After a while they realised that the security guard was singing. What was obviously once a light, poppy love song had mutated into something harsh, sinister and portentous. It echoed on the stone walls of the precinct as if rumbling up from the bowels of the earth. Jimmy quite liked it:

'Run baby run
Run to the sun
Just give me the word
We'll go free as a bird
In the blue ooh ooh sky

Run baby run baby RUN!'

He had obviously not been the singer for The Shoemakers.

'1968 – you ask them. Look at me now eh?' He paused for breath. 'I shouldn't really tell you this, but I know a good place where you can put up your posters.'

After taking directions to a prime sight, thanking him profusely and, especially Jimmy, promising to look up The Shoemakers, they moved on. As she passed him the security guard took Emma's arm and held her back.

'You know what you've got to do? You know what my advice would be?'

The receding group had moved a long way off. They were little more than dots at the end of the vast, concrete concourse. Emma could still make out Tzannis though, that waddling, flat-footed gait of his.

152

'I ended up as a security guard because I wasn't hard enough. It's a cut-throat world, the music business. It's been obvious to you for weeks. He's the only one who doesn't fit in, he's too domestic, too safe. You love him to bits, but there's a personality clash there, him and Donald, him and Paul, he just doesn't hit it off with either of them. That's right. You've got to lose the Greek.'

Another hour and they had used up all the posters. By this time all was harmony again. Trading fantasies as they pasted, they had worked themselves into a fever pitch of expectation. Over coffee at Emma's flat they discussed how long they should leave it before putting up the next, more detailed posters, what they should wear for the gig, who they should invite. Tzannis wanted to discuss making more time for rehearsals and some ideas he'd had about "jazzing up" the few numbers they had. It amused them, that phrase, "jazzing up". Emma thought it sounded like something you do to a sitting room, not a song. Paul wanted to know what Tzannis was going to wear. He hadn't really given it much thought. Jimmy hoped that Donald's head was better, and when Paul suggested that it had been a rather fortuitous ailment he was soundly chastised by Emma.

They drank coffee for an hour or so, Jimmy tossing them scraps from his Fantasy on the Theme of a Meteoric Rise to Fame, which they fell on and devoured with gusto. Then they went their separate ways.

Tzannis felt unaccountably blue on the way back to The Olive Tree. But rather than dwell on it he turned the feeling in to a riff – he wasn't altogether happy with it, but it had the makings of something. Then he could hear the riff coming to him from the wind that was now blowing through the fence above the underpass. This often happened. Tzannis would imagine music, then apply it to some external force – the noise of traffic, the ticking of a particular clock, the sound of machinery, bird song – and allow that to influence it, to play it back to him. Though he wasn't aware of it yet, this instinctive method was a unique and precious gift. He would certainly never have tried to explain it to the others.

Paul had the longest walk home, out to the suburbs where he still lived with his mother and father. As he rounded the corner he noticed that the living room light was still on.

'I don't believe it. Mum.'

Exasperated, he leant back against a lamp post to have one more fag and contemplate the burdens of leadership.

'Waiting up for you?'

The voice had come from the privet bushes behind him. He turned to see a pair of feet poking out from under the nearest bush.

'Sorry lad, didn't mean to make you jump,' said the bush, 'what's the bucket and brush for?'

'I've been putting up posters.'

'Ah, an artiste!'

He caught a strong waft of cheap spirits.

'I'm in a band.'

'I was an artiste once, a performance poet. A performance poet, I ask you, what a farce. Is there any other kind? And do you know what happened, do you know why I . . . ' The bush rustled fiercely as the speaker finished off the sentence with an expansive gesture. 'Because, because, my fine young artiste, I was shit!'

Like a fish breaking the surface of a choppy lake, a head emerged from the bush, then sunk slowly back in. Paul couldn't make out the features, just a texture – rough, bristled, leathery. 'Shit, shit, shit, shit . . .' said the voice weakly as it faded back into the bushes, and then, more stridently, 'shall I give you a recitation?':

'You, you got to do the right thing
Even when the world's saying no
Even when your head's saying go.'

Paul decided that the safest thing was to say nothing and walk away. As he walked the voice moved alongside him behind the hedges and fences. Paul recognised the "poem" as the lyrics to a song that Mysterical had been working on in his garage just the week before. His lyrics.

Paul increased his speed. But the voice kept up with him:

'Go go go
You gotta stay
Don't go away
You gotta stay
With what really matters.'

'Not really poetry, is it,' said the voice, 'it's just doggerel, it's just shit.'

Paul told the voice to leave him alone, but it started to sing now. Still those lyrics of his, but to the tune of 'Run Baby Run' by The Shoemakers. The chorus fitted perfectly, a chorus that he had been particularly proud of:

'Friends and lovers
Lovers and friends
That's the kind of trust
That never ends.'

Paul lost it. He screamed at the hedge to shut up.

'You're just weak,' he bellowed, 'weak, weak, weak. So fucking weak!'

For the first time ever he swore at his mother when he got in. She instantly assumed that he'd been taking drugs. His father was roused and there was a row.

When Paul eventually got to his room he pulled out those lyrics and did a radical rewrite. Stuff about "the ends justifying the means", how you've got to "break a few eggs to make an omelette" - it took him a while to find a rhyme with "omelette" – and the importance of "looking out for number one".

Heard of a band called Mysterical?

Unlikely. They only played three gigs, and none of them were particularly well attended. The original line-up changed after the first gig and that was the death of them. The female lead singer was replaced by a sixteen-year-old art student who couldn't hold a tune or sing a note and was in a permanent state of bitter conflict with the song writer – it seems that she wrote songs too and considered hers superior, which they probably were. The Greek bass player, who had given them a truly original sound, lost his place to a good-looking young man who'd done a performing arts course and knew all about "stage presence". He could play reasonably well but never turned up for rehearsals. A further nail in the coffin was their treatment at the hands of a con man, who claimed to be the former manager of a well-known band. Mysterical gave him a substantial amount of money to produce a demo tape, which, needless to say, never materialised. An attempt to retrieve the cash resulted in the guitarist/song writer's mother receiving a number of threatening phone calls.

The ousted Greek became a highly successful session musician. His sinuous bass lines, combining his cultural influences with rhythms from the urban environment, are constantly in demand from the world's top artists.

Emma and Paul bumped in to one another some years later in another city, they were both surprised to see how smartly the other was dressed. He was in insurance, she was working for the Inland Revenue. They both seemed happy with their lot.

They went to a cafe – a Greek one, ironically enough – and laughed about how ridiculous the whole thing had been.

'We were good though, weren't we?'

'Oh yes, given the breaks I'm sure we could have made it. It's like anything, it's not *what* you know, it's *who* you know.'

'Regrets?'

'No, not really. But I do think we listened to some bad advice.'

And just like old times they sat there watching people making faces at themselves in the window.

Editor's Choice

I was brought up in South Wales and Yorkshire, before fleeing to New Zealand where I had a longer than expected holiday romance. Ten years later I am still on holiday! I have made up stories ever since I can remember, mainly to get me out of trouble and to escape real life. I then progressed to angst-ridden poetry in my teens. Five years ago I gave it up to start writing seriously. In my spare time I earn a living as a psychotherapist and work with people who are perched precariously on the line of sanity. I have had stories published in several NZ and Australian literary magazines, won a NZ short story competition and had a story included in the *Penguin NZ New Fiction Anthology*. I have spent two long arduous years writing my first novel. I am just about to re-write it for the third time.

The No Thumb Hitch-Hiker

Sarah Weir

The Dakota wilderness was so vast it pushed its way inside my mind and stretched it out, like a giant Atlas straining against two closing walls. In the midst of this elongation, the clutter sank to the floor, leaving me with a stark view of who I was, and what my life was all about. Cass was driving, strangely silent, as we snaked down the sheer mountains towards the quivering prairies below. I was in a deep tarmac trance. By the end of the day I was shedding clutter by the side of the road, leaving behind what I didn't like until I was pared down to the bare essentials.

I didn't see him until we were right up close. He resembled a turtle stumbling along the roadside. The dusty shell of his pack bent his back, while his neck protruded forwards. He stared at the ground, fixing his eyes on the dust, meditating on each particle as they splattered his boots a cracked white. I registered him for a brief moment as we passed. There were no towns for miles to come. Only the odd farmhouse, tucked in an elbow of mountain, silent and staring. Hidden beneath his pack, he was nondescript against the black-tipped peaks and sulphurous, brooding forests. His stoop, his stumbling plod had an air of penitence, as if he was embarked on a pilgrimage. We fixed our eyes on him, fascinated, and then forgot him, like so many things we passed.

Cass suddenly pulled into a moccasin tourist shop, with a fibreglass wigwam in the front yard. Before I could follow she was inside, interrogating the shopkeeper about the cultural homicide of Native Americans.

"But why don't you 'ave any books about thim. You're just milking thur culture. Selling plastic arrows isn't culture yer know. I want to read summat that really tells me about thim. Yer know, like what's really in thur minds, when they're sitting round t'fire. What they talk about like." The balding shopkeeper looked blank. Her Rotherham dialect might have been Japanese for all he could understand of it. Let alone wanting to understand those pig-ignorant redskin bums.

Cass, in her frustration, decided we needed a beer. Shortly after we stopped at a bar at the side of the road. One or two houses clustered round its sides. There were few signs of life. The barman was polishing glasses. We could hear the hum of fans as he poured our beers.

Cass stared furiously at a gaudy set of oil paintings on the far wall, featuring naked braves with red demonic eyes, bearing down on fallen buffalo, and doleful squaws with eyes fixed on the horizon, as if their only thought was looking epic.

"Injuns killed all the buffalo," commented the barman, his red sweaty hair glued to his forehead.

"Only according to John Wayne," I said grimly. He shrugged. "Still, plenty left to hunt round here. We ain't short. You've got your bear, your mountain lion, your coyote, your moose, now they're nice over a spit . . ." The list seemed endless. To interrupt, we ordered a large plate of steak and fries.

The door swung open. The turtled pilgrim hobbled to the bar, his back still bent beneath the rucksack. His face was streaked with rivulets of dust and sweat. The barman moved over.

"What'll you have?" he asked. "Looks like you been walkin' a mighty long way." The man didn't answer immediately. He took out a neat, white pressed handkerchief and mopped his brow, carefully folding it back into his top pocket. Then he fished out some change. I noticed his fingers were long and thin, the nails manicured into the shape of shells. When he'd counted his money, he looked up and asked for a beer, thanking the barman several times as it was poured.

"Where you come from?" the barman asked.

"Hector," the man said.

"Hector, why thas miles."

"Didn't get me no rides t'day. Sometimes it's like that." We could tell now, the motionless whisper was shaping itself into a Texan accent.

Cass leaned over. She could never keep herself out of other people's conversations. She wormed herself in, writing her own invitations.

"We would of given you a lift, if we'd known you wanted one. But you didn't 'ave yer thumb out."

"Never do," the man said turning to her, lifting up his beer. "Reckon, people wanna give a lift they do. If they don't, they don't. No point in pushin' it."

Cass was incredulous. "But 'ow the 'eck is anyone s'posed to know you want a ride, if your thumb ain't out? We just thought you were on a walking holiday. Enjoying it like. Ee, you'll niver git rides like that." She shook her head, draining her beer. She hated people who made their lives difficult. "There's enough crosses in life without 'aving to go and nail yourself up to one," she said to me once, driven crazy by her Mum's persistent martyrdom.

The No Thumb Hitch-hiker held out an immaculate hand. His skin brushed against me like a ripple of silk.

"Name's Easter McClure. No kiddin'," he said in response to our dubious looks. "Born on Easter see. Used to it now. Was kinda rough in school an' all that."

Cass drew up her bar stool, so she was next to his. "So anyhow, you on holiday or something?"

"I have a month on the road every year. Jus' wanderin' where the wind or the rides take me. Gettin' the feel of God's country. An' his people. Like you fine ladies." A shy smile trickled across his face. "Got me a busy life at home. I own an oil drillin' station down in Texas, an' a ranch. Spend ma whole time on the phone, in meetins, buyin', sellin' . . . I like havin' this time to contemplate." He looked up and I saw his eyes. They shone a fervent blue, astonishing against his small-featured, dust-cracked face. "I'm fixin' to go home directly. Business calls. You ladies should come by. Got plenty o' horses. You ride?"

We both nodded. "Well you should drop on by. We're havin' a rodeo at the end of the month. Half o' Texas will be there."

"I still don't get it, if you don't mind me saying," Cass was persistent. "Why on foot, doing it the hard way."

"It reminds me of what's important in life. In case I fergit. I nearly forgot it once, an' lost somethin' precious."

A moth flew in from the dusk. Our stools were huddled round the bar. Easter was enjoying the small pool of limelight. Cass and I listened to his stories, telling him our own in return.

"Ma father, he was a preacher. Baptist. Stern man. Times were hard, preachin' in Texas. When th' oil came, people jus' went crazy over the money. They installed giant satellite dishes. Once they were connected to MTV, they had no need for God. I was lucky. Fell in love. Her family had money. We bought some land and began drillin' jus' like everyone else. Only we hit it big time. Had oil spillin' out of our ears."

He told us the story of his life, with his slow plodding accent, as if unaware of its impossible nature, staring us straight in the eye, no traces of shiftiness or facade in his face.

"They say God moves in mysterious ways. Well, I'm convinced of that maself. Got too big and mighty for ourselves. The biggest swimmin' pool, barbecue, limos . . . none of it satisfied us. We kept feelin' empty and fillin' up the space with whiskey. Course, it couldn't last. She was fixin' to leave. Only jus' before, we were drivin' home one night. Car hit a rut and . . ." his voice had a slight tremble, "we jus' rolled into a ditch. She weren't wearin' no seat belt. Killed right out."

He took off his shoes and showed us the blisters on his feet. "This is so I never forget. I can't turn my back on the ranch. But I ain't turnin my back on the Lord no more."

I had the feeling he was inventing himself as he went along. Hobo or millionaire, it was hard to tell. But even it was only a story, it was a good story. He was turning himself into a myth.

Easter bought us another round, counting out the last of the change and laying it across the bar.

"So what about you girls, whad're you here for?"

"We're just travelling," Cass said. "You know, 'aving a bit of a laugh." We didn't tell him that we'd just buried Cass's mother, riddled with cancer from breathing in her Dad's cigarette smoke in that cramped terrace house all those years. That beer made Cass hurl rocks at trees. There was a tree for God, one for the Church, one for her Dad and then an indiscriminate number for all those people (this included ourselves) who had money, and lived as an unbearable comparison to her mother's drab existence.

She was getting irritated with Easter. For doing things the hard way. And because she thought she was being conned. She gazed obliquely at the gaudy Indians when he tried to meet her eyes.

"So where you girls fixin' to stay the night?" Lennie the barman asked, leaning over the bar, smirking mysteriously.

"Dunno," I said. "Hadn't thought that far. We sleep in t'car."

"There's a campsite up the road. It's by a crick. Lovely lil place."

He gave us directions, and made us promise to return his way in the morning. "Nothin' like eggs easy over to settle a stomach for the road." We looked at the stooped, dust-riddled creature hunched on the stool. He stared down at the floor, as if trying to melt himself into the furniture. Cass rolled her eyes, with her spare-me look.

"D'you want to come with us, t'campsite?" she asked.

"Why Mam, if it ain't no bother to you fine ladies."

"Oh no," I said. "No bother like." Cass pulled another face.

Easter got in beside Cass, who was downing the bottle of Wild Turkey. I focussed my blurred eyes on the rutted track, as I drove us through the woods to the campsite. The dark branches seethed, like giant, grasping claws.

Cass found a pile of firewood stacked by a fire pit. She began chopping it.

"Here, let me do that," Easter said, standing up.

"It's alright," Cass said, swinging the axe above her head. "Reckon thas more of a man's-size axe."

The axe crashed through the wood in a swift, splintering slice.

"Really," Cass said lifting the axe again.

Easter sat and watched her uncomfortably. I poured us all a whiskey and handed him one. "'Aven't you heard of girl power?" Cass asked. "We're very combat trousers round 'ere you know."

"And I got me Brownie Guides firelighting badge," I said, collecting some twigs. "Practised at 'ome in me living room."

We perched on logs drinking whiskey. Easter looked baffled. He didn't say no to the whiskey though. After a while, he suddenly sat up, his body stiff and alert. "Listen," he said. "Coyote." In the distance we could hear an eerie howl. Closer than that, behind our backs, was a strange rustling.

"It's a pack. They've got us surrounded," Easter said, his voice a grave whisper.

"Where?" Cass was suspicious. "I can't see anything."

"You won't. They hide in the bushes. We won't even hear 'em come."

"So how d'you know they're there then?" I asked.

"Always one who howls, jus' before the attack."

"We seen plenty of coyote, while we've been sitting round t'fire. How come they niver attacked us then?"

"By themselves, they alright. It's when they're in a pack."

"Like Sheffield United fans, you mean?"

Easter blinked at her, his blue eyes watery and bemused in the firelight. More howls echoed through the blackness. The bushes were fervid with whispering leaves.

"So, what do we do?" I asked Easter.

"It's tricky," he said. "They go for movement. We're safer when we're still. But to be real safe, we need to get inside the car. Give me the keys and I'll see if I can make it to the car. Then I'll roll it backwards down to where you are."

We were both silent. Just as I was about to say it, Cass's voice came curtly out of the darkness. "I'm sorry mate, no one gets the car keys 'cept us. I'll go."

"No," Easter insisted, his voice sounding panicky. "You girls don't realise. I was out fishin' with a good friend of mine, an' we got surrounded just like this. I tole ma friend not to move, but he panicked. They pounced on him. It was a terrible sight. His screams the worst. Still got me nightmares 'bout that. Did everythin' I could, but they were in a blood frenzy. Never gonna fergit that moment. I have to go. You ladies must understand. I couldn't live with someone else's blood on ma hands."

"I'll go," I said to Cass.

"No, this one's mine," she said easing her hand forward and clasping the axe firmly. She moved infinitesimally towards the car.

"I'm sorry," I said to Easter. "But we do things for ourselves round here. Deprived childhoods you see, and Margaret Thatcher." He blinked again, another wall of bewilderment descending. "I'm sorry about your friend," I added.

As I stared into the darkness I saw two red pinpricks. I rubbed my eyes. The pinpricks disappeared. Then a constellation of red stars swam before me, scattered through the bushes.

"Jesus, Easter," I said. "You got me seeing things now."

"You're seeing them eyes, ain't you?"

"How the fuck did you know that?"

"I tole you, they're all around us."

Cass rolled the car down to where we were sitting. I inched my way in the hatchback door, followed by Easter. We slammed it behind us. Sealing out the danger. Or sealing it in. I wasn't sure which.

Cass and I climbed fully clothed into our sleeping bags and lay on the mattress in the back of the station wagon. Easter arranged himself across the front seats. I noticed that Cass had kept hold of the axe. I felt underneath for the kitchen knife we kept close by. Cass exacted her revenge with a rave about life in Rotherham, that went into the early hours. Most of it went over Easter's head. He'd never even seen Coronation Street, so he didn't get "going down t'local, t'chippie, t'footie", let alone the miners' strike and class consciousness. That was fine with Cass. She was fired up with whiskey and was busy rewriting her past in red ink. Eventually the polite hmms from the front seat were silent. We allowed ourselves to close our eyes. I slept fitfully despite the whiskey, listening to every squeak and rustle that came from inside and out.

I was woken by a thump on the bonnet. I opened my eyes. The light was grey and dim. A jay had crash-landed on the car and was pecking at the windscreen wiper. The front seat was empty. I looked around. Our belongings remained intact. My money still in my pockets. Cass was asleep beside me. I nudged her.

"Cass, he's gone." She sat up, eyes wide open.

"Anything nicked?"

"The whiskey's gone."

"Did you believe all that crap about coyotes?"

"Not for a minute. What about you?"

"Na. Man's got a bigger gob than a roomful of Gazza's."

We reached Lennie's somewhat later that morning. The whiskey had taken its toll. Lennie brought us large mugs of coffee.

"What happened to that lil guy?"

"Dunno," Cass said. "He tried to steal our car and then buggered off."

"Still," I said, "he kept us well entertained."

Lennie's toilets were in a lean-to, at the side of the bar. As I was sitting there, I heard the familiar Texan drawl, using the payphone just outside.

"Hank . . . How y'all doing down there? You truckin' up those cattle today, like I said . . . yeah I know about that . . . you tole me . . . but if you don't box 'em up soon, price is gonna drop . . . we got one, two days max . . . yeah I know the boys're gettin' restless . . . sure well wouldn't you . . . they're sittin twiddlin' their thumbs til you git this thing fixed up . . . "

Cass was incredulous. "Well berloody hell. I thought he wos telling big porkies."

I thought of the eyes glowing red in the dark.

Lennie came over with the pot of coffee.

"We just heard the No Thumb Hitch-hiker outside. He was calling home. Seems like he does own a ranch an' all," Cass said.

"Well, I don' know about that," Lennie said, a wry smile crossing his white, chubby face, pouring coffee into my mug. "That phone ain't bin workin' ever since the boys pissed in it last Thanksgivin'. I think Buddy shoved his beertop inside . . . thought he was gonna have free calls all the way to Alaska . . . those boys . . ." He shook his head.

We didn't see Easter that day as we drove out of the mountains. I kept looking for him, his turtle-hunched body, but he had vanished, as if he had reinvented himself as the elements themselves. Out on the prairies the sky was vast. It shone like fervent blue eyes, windswept and prophetic .

Stella Galea

Editor's Choice

Was born in South London. She still lives there and works as a manager for the UK Nursing Council. She keeps writing short stories. She tries to stay out of the way.

Life Assurance

Stella Galea

One of the theories about the universe says that it is mostly dark matter. You can't see dark matter and they don't know what it's made of except that it's probably stuff left over from the beginning of time. Dark matter hangs around in space exerting a gravitational pull without which the universe would be free to expand into infinity. Some believe that our own Milky Way is hurtling through space at a stomach-churning speed, drawn toward a web of dark matter where we will eventually be caught in a tangle of galaxies. Finally, in a few billion years when all the galaxies are piled up in one great dark matter junkyard the universe will go crunch and there will be an end to it. At least, that's the theory.

Blake was falling from an unimaginable height. He woke with a racing heart just before hitting the ground to find that he had dozed off in front of Saturday afternoon television. The unseasonal sunshine which had previously lit the pale London day had disappeared, darkening the sky while a blustery wind began to blow. Unable to shake off the dream he flicked on a lamp and turned off the TV. He was thinking about going to the kitchen to get a beer when there was a knock at the door.

The man on the doorstep was priest-like in his long dark coat over a white collarless shirt. As the door opened he raised his head and looked at Blake. In middle age or maybe a little older he had black hair that touched his shoulders and striking pale skin. He raised a hand to shake Blake's at the same time as a fork of lightning backlit the sky giving the impressive effect that he had commanded it.

"Mr Blake," he said without seeming to move his lips. "How secure is your future? What would you do if an accident rendered you unfit to work? Would you like to be rich? Mr Blake, do you expect Jesus to save you?"

"Look, I'm not really . . ."

"Thank you, that's kind," said the man entering the house with an elegant sweep of his coat. He was already in the living room when he turned to Blake, left standing at the door. He focussed an intensely expectant stare on him.

"What on earth do you want from your life, Mr Blake? What can you possibly expect? What?"

"I er . . . Are you a Jehovah's Witness? I'm not interested."

"Answer my question."

"I've already got a . . ."

"A what? Do you think I'm selling something? Then you've got it wrong."

Just as Blake was beginning to feel threatened he realised it was just some besuited salesman with split ends and shoes scuffed from walking the city streets. To confirm it the man said quietly, "Insurance, Mr Blake. Just insurance."

"How do you know my name?"

"Off your doorbell," he said quickly.

"Well, actually, I've got Contents already and I can't really afford any more."

The man said, "Do you mind if I sit down? It's my leg. I was in the war."

"Which one?"

"Oh, you know." The man eased himself into a chair. "All of them. Now, Mr Blake. Tell me. What do you desire most in your life?"

A brief and lovely image of Amina from Business Systems crossed his mind and he replied, "Financial security."

The visitor smiled an icy smile. "Then I can offer you an absolutely unique, once-in-a-lifetime deal. I can offer you a regular monthly income as well as a substantial lump sum."

"I haven't got anything to invest. I can barely pay the mortgage. I don't want to waste your time."

"I promise you that this is an offer that you can easily afford. Indeed, can't afford to turn down." He gazed at Blake with an almost loving intensity. "We undertake to pay into your account a tax-free sum on a monthly basis as well as a generous lump sum as I mentioned before. Furthermore as a special customer you are entitled to gifts, let's say bonuses at regular, unspecified intervals. And here's where we blow you away," he beamed a business-school beam. "During the term of the policy you don't have to pay a penny. Not a penny."

Blake waited for the catch. It was some new scam. You got a couple of TV licence stamps and the occasional free biro and all you had to do was buy ten thousand pounds' worth of double glazing. "OK. So how much do I get a month?"

The visitor's face clouded. He said slowly, "Whatever you desire."

"Er. Can I see some ID?"

"Certainly." He took out a wallet which at first glance appeared to be made of the skin of some rare reptile but was actually just plastic. He snapped it open and produced a business card which he handed to Blake. He could have sworn it read 'Satan, Prince of Air and Darkness, Harvester of Souls' but looking again he realised it was simply 'Nick Smith, Financial Adviser'. "At your service sir."

Blake began to get annoyed. "But you're not just going to hand over all this stuff for nothing. I have to pay something."

"Of course. Everything has a price. As has everyone. But the price of this deal is not paid until the term of the policy has elapsed. The term of the policy is twenty-four years. Nothing to pay until one score and four years has passed."

"But how much? Can't you tell me that?"

"I've got a schedule. Here in my briefcase." Blake hadn't noticed the case that sat at Nick Smith's feet. He picked it up and balanced it on his knee to open it. "You can look at this in your own time. But I can assure you that what we require you already have."

Blake looked at Nick Smith and he began to feel a little sick. He couldn't escape the impression that his face was constantly changing as if his age, demeanour and even features were completely fluid. He blinked the impression away. "I don't believe it. It doesn't make any sense."

Nick Smith leaned forward conspiratorially. "But what if it were true? Wouldn't you be interested? Wouldn't you?"

Blake shifted in his seat. He laughed nervously. "Well. As much money as I want and nothing to pay for twenty-four years. Of course I'd be interested."

He thought about never having to work again. Never having to worry about the roof or the damp. He thought about Amina from Business Systems next to him on a warm Mediterranean night counting the stars and tracking the travelling moon. Oh for Christ sake the man was a con man.

"I promise you I will never lie to you Blake. Let me prove that you can trust me."

He placed the briefcase on the coffee table, opened it and with a theatrical gesture he turned it to face Blake. The case contained fifty-pound notes. More money than Blake had ever seen. All tidily bound in packs, just like in a kidnap film.

Blake laughed. "That's not real, that's just fake."

The visitor's eyes flared. "Why should I waste my time? Here, have it anyway."

And Blake took a packet of notes and pulled one out of the middle. He hadn't seen many fifties but by all the ways he could judge it looked real.

"But I don't understand. What do you get at the end of twenty-four years that could possibly be worth your while?"

"Well. Just have a quick read of this. It ought to explain everything."

He handed him four sheets of manuscript, closely typed in narrow columns which reminded Blake of his mortgage offer. It began, "Subject to any contractual provisions to the contrary Brimstone Investments herein known as the Party in the First Part undertakes to uphold and fulfil in full and in total the articles and obligations (as the case may be) contained in schedule 17 part 3 i, ii and iii subject to the provisions of (and without prejudice to) clause 16 in respect of the Client herein known as the Party in Second Part."

"What . . ." said Blake. "What?"

"What's the matter? It's perfectly plain isn't it? Anyway you can skip to the last paragraph."

Blake read, "Clause 26. The Party in the Second Part does undertake, subject to the provisions of the contract mentioned above, to tender unto the Party in the First Part the sum described in clause 27 at the end of the term agreed. Payment shall be made in full at the time, or shortly after, the expiry of the Party in the Second Part.

"Um. Clause 27. Payment shall consist of the whole and complete portion of the animating or essential substance or substances. No payment in kind will be accepted."

Blake looked up from the page ". . . animating or essential substance? I don't get it."

Nick Smith sighed. "You don't pay a thing for twenty-four years. In twenty-four years you die and I get what's left."

"You mean, like my house?"

"Not like your house," he spat. "Listen to what I'm saying to you."

Nick Smith's shifting features grew bold and pronounced as if outlined by an artist in oils, he became a creature with eyes of kaleidoscoping colours and translucent skin. He seemed to Blake to grow taller, statelier, radiant. Blake felt a thrill as if he were in the presence of something holy. He felt himself vanishing into the salesman's magnetic presence.

"Understand me. Believe me. I have chosen you and I will give you everything beyond your wildest imaginings. You will have power, wealth, any woman you desire, the answer to any mystery. Think of it. Any material thing you desire will be yours. All I want is the immaterial."

Blake stared at him. "Wait a minute. You want my soul?"

Nick Smith smiled, shimmering with the old power. "At last."

The smile melted as Blake's shoulders started shaking in an insolent giggle. "What is this? Are we being filmed? Is it for TV or something?"

Nick Smith roared, "You think this is funny. You'll go into your coffin laughing and then what. What do you believe? In your TV? In Elvis? I can see the soul you don't believe you have and it's as good as mine already. So laugh. You puny mortal."

"Did you just call me a puny mortal? Excellent."

"I could kill you with a thought."

Nick Smith appeared to Blake to mutate to become the ancient horned creature of fire, he seemed to grow to the height of the ceiling and wider than the bounds of the room. Blake knew he was mistaken in what he believed he saw and he shut his eyes. Looking again he was back facing the insurance man with the somewhat elaborate patter. Of course. What else would he see?

Nick Smith made an irritated sigh and snatched the contract away. For the first time Blake noticed that he was quite a small and stooped man with clasping hands, darting eyes and a nervous way about him.

"Look mate," said Nick Smith. "I'll be straight with you. If I don't make my quota I'm out of a job. I haven't sold a policy in days. Do me a favour. It's just a fiver a month for ten years, then you get it back with a bit of interest on top. I'm sorry about before. All this money's fake. Company promotion sort of thing. Know what I mean?"

Blake again felt a wave of nausea. "A fiver. Yeah sure. I'll take it, if you just leave."

Nick Smith brightened. "Really? OK. You just have to sign here." He pointed to the bottom line of the same contract.

"Have you got a pen?"

"Actually you have to sign in blood," Nick Smith looked sheepish. "Your own blood. Company policy. Don't ask me why. If you sign in blood you get Marks and Spencer vouchers."

"Oh come on. Get out. You're one of those insane people."

Nick Smith seemed to stand once more and once more attain a great height. He raised his hands and the room seemed to become a mountain and he and Blake were standing on a ledge overlooking the whole world.

"Blake. I have power. 'To make the moon drop from her sphere or the ocean to overwhelm the world.' All this. Just imagine for a minute."

Blake turned to him. "What is this? How did you do it? Did you give me some drugs or something?"

And then they were back facing each other in the living room. Nick Smith seemed to have grown smaller, a little lost in his coat. Standing, he shut the briefcase fumbling over the clasps. "Good evening," he said and without another word he left the house.

Blake looked at the fifty-pound note that he still held in his hand. "That was weird," he said and, still shaken from his dream of falling, he went to the kitchen to get a beer.

Satan, Prince of Air and Darkness, Harvester of Souls walked down the garden path and out into the street. "Damn the twentieth century," he muttered. "They just don't get it. No fun any more."

He stopped by a tree-dotted wasteground where Blake's street met three others. Gusts of wind grabbed autumn leaves to lay down a carpet before him and he looked at the sky. No stars. Not even true darkness in this city.

He raised a hand and the gales grew until the people in the houses at the crossroads heard the whistling like the moaning of a lost child and their windows shook and burglar alarms shrieked and they shivered and turned up their central heating. Then the Prince walked slowly with immense dignity into the wasteland.

Another theory goes that in ten billion years or so no one will care about the tempting attractions of dark matter. By then the stars will have burnt out the last of the big bang energy and will spark out one by one. The universe will simply lose interest and switch itself off and there will be an end to it. At least, that's the theory.

Editor's Choice

All I can say for definite is that at twenty-four, I am old enough to know
that cigarettes are bad for me.

Wardrobe

Patrick O'Toole

Cheese took his hands away from his ears. They hurt. His ears that is, not his hands. Stinging kind of hurt, not pain hurt. He had flattened them against the side of his head with the palms of his hands and he had forgotten it would hurt when he stopped. That was the only way it worked though. If he didn't press hard enough he could still hear the noise from downstairs penetrating the barrier his hands made. Same old screaming match, same old ding-dong. Cheese liked that, ding-dong, his grandmother used to say it a lot. Another day, Eamon, same old ding-dong. Cheese heard another shout, but his ears hurt too much, so he just let his head fall back to rest on the sheet of wood that was the side of the wardrobe. He closed his eyes. Sometimes, if you couldn't see something you didn't hear it so well.

be quiet, you'll wake the kids

It was his mother, although Cheese could barely hear her. She wasn't shouting.

fuck the kids

His father was definitely shouting.

stop that, please, the children, they're . . .

and Cheese heard a pause, he heard the silence,

they're only children

Cheese liked the way the dull nothing vacuum of hands against

179

ears sounded of nothing. It was like being underwater, in the bath with your head under the water and your fingers pinching your nose, a different world. A different, silent one. But then there would be the sound of something breaking and the vibration, the sheer vehemence of destruction would make him resurface, a glass against a wall maybe, or a plate, or a chair too violently kicked. One morning Cheese came downstairs and found the glass door of the oven, the inner one, shattered around the floor of the kitchen. In pieces everywhere. He spent the day wondering how they had managed to break it and yet leave the outer door intact. It was good in a way, a puzzle to occupy his mind, better than double science and trying to concentrate on first-year biology. Secondary school was harder than primary and double science first thing on a Tuesday morning was definitely the most boring hour and a half of the week, and Mrs Hallissey had a mole on her face that made Cheese sick just to look at it. It was bad enough being bored, without having to look at that as well. A big jungle of wiry hair that just sat there and behaved itself. *Hairy* someone in the classroom would exclaim, disguising it as a cough, *face* answered an anonymous voice from the far side of the room. No one would snigger or giggle or anything, *hairy . . . face,* everyone would just wait with elbows on tables and hands tucked under chins, wait and wait. *Hairy . . . face.* The first couple of times it happened, Mrs Hallissey had turned around in disbelief and embarrassment and searched for words. A red face, a big red face with a wig wannabe prospering where it shouldn't. Now though, she did nothing. She just kept writing at the blackboard not acknowledging anything, and the whole class stared at her back, watching her shoulder blades quivering with the effort of pressing chalk against board, bang, scrape, bang and scrape, PHOTOSYNTHESIS, CHLOROPHYLL . . . Everyone waited for her to do something, anything. Do something Mrs H., *for fuck sake do something.*

Double science was only good when something out of the

ordinary happened, something to break the routine. The day they had done the sex education chapter in the biology book. Chapter eight. Mrs Hallissey was reading aloud, and everyone was waiting for the third page. She finally got there and read over the word *penis* without looking up. Everyone, boys and girls, smiled. Or didn't smile but wanted to. One girl giggled though and suddenly the whole class was hysterical, screaming. Everyone just erupted, the absurd noise the word made just hanging in the air the way a bad smell does, or a canned air freshener to mask a bad smell does. It just wasn't a spoken word. You could read it to yourself okay, but no one ever said it. It was ridiculous: penis, PENIS. Cheese had enjoyed those few minutes, the sanctity of the word somehow excusing the class of misbehaviour. Mrs Hallissey had reddened and shouted for order.

Show us yours Miss

someone shouted from the back, securely anonymous in the mayhem, and someone else threw a sandwich at her desk. Cheese thought that was a bit too much.

a penis sandwich

It hit her on the neck and the chalk in her hand snapped and scraped against the board. Organ became Orgay as the whole class was suddenly aware that they had gone too far. Much too far. Sometimes Cheese hated being a child. All the time actually. Cheese didn't like people giving Mrs. Hallissey a hard time. He thought she was nice. Soft eyes.

Leave her alone

He had fallen asleep in the classroom one day, and instead of getting angry, and shouting, and ranting, and pointing, she just brought him to the staffroom and offered him a glass of milk. The staffroom was bigger than Cheese had imagined it, and it smelt of cigarettes and wet coats. And feet.

How's your mother Eamon, you know we went to school together don't you?

She's fine Miss

And your father, is he still only working part-time ?
Yes Miss

The milk was warm, Cheese didn't really like it unless it was just out of the fridge, warm milk tasted sour and left a scum in your mouth.

And were you up late last night Eamon?

Cheese knew it was coming, he had been waiting for it, reprimand and punishment. He had once seen a television programme about a country where they flogged people. Tied them and whipped them.

No Miss

The glass was dirty as well. Cheese could see two fingerprints near the rim. It had probably been washed in cold water. His mother had taught Cheese how to wash glasses, it wasn't like just washing plates or knives and forks. You had to wash the glasses first while the water was still clean. And then you had to give them a quick rinse under the tap before leaving them to drain.

Well, I think you'll have to start getting to bed a little earlier, won't you Eamon?

Yes Miss

And that was it. Over. Yes Miss, thank you miss, yes miss, yesmiss, yezmiz. A reprieve, relief, that was it. No shouting or saliva, or fingers, or ultimatums. That was it. Cheese definitely liked her. Her wrinkles were kind. He couldn't tell anyone he liked her of course, they would just give him grief. He would get hounded at lunchtime forever.

Cheese and Hairyface up a tree, K.I.S.S.I.N.G.
First comes love, then comes marriage
then comes a baby in a carriage

They were still young enough for baby rhymes. And just old enough for innuendo.

didya givver one Cheese? didya? didya givver one?

Bastards.

But at least the time passed quicker when there was some excitement during double science. Especially when his mind could give its attention to something very different, like the oven door, or the guy on that special programme at Christmas who could turn a tennis ball inside out. Without cutting it anywhere. No cut, no puncture, nothing. Amazing. *Class.*

Cheese clamped his hands back on his ears, it hadn't finished after all. The shouting. His dad must have been lighting a cigarette, probably not though, there hadn't been a *where the fuck are my cigarettes?*

Whereermefuckinfags? the fuck are my cigarettes ?

I don't know, I haven't seen them

when I leave something somewhere I spect it to stay where it was left, is that reasonable, am I being reasonable? am I not being reasonable?

Each word was exquisitely pronounced through the beer slur. Cheese's father was trying hard with his diction. Concentrating even.

And then it stopped again.

They were probably just taking a break. Grown-ups do that all the time. Cheese knew the pattern by heart. They would be talking, and then they would just stop for a while. Or his mother would be washing dishes at the sink, her yellow marigold hands moving in and out of the water, in out up down plate wipe rinse plate, and then she would just stop. Stop. And her head would drop and her hands would sit there in the foaming basin, and she would shake very slightly. Cheese had been sitting at the table one day feeding his younger sister. *Come on Em, open up, come on, please, please Emma look, look it's so good so nice.* And Cheese would eat some of it from the strangely shaped super safe plastic spoon and try so so hard to hide his grimace. It was awful, it didn't taste of anything. Cheese was glad he couldn't remember being Emma's age. Everything she ate was from a box, it was always powder from a box, and then it got mixed with warm water and it was suddenly food. Pretend food. *Come on Em, open up.* But she wouldn't, and Cheese had looked up to ask his mother to do it. He stopped himself though, because she didn't look right, just standing there, shaking ever so slightly, and not really doing anything. Nothing in the kitchen was moving, and the kitchen was never still, there was always something happening. It was always dirty, or getting dirty, or clean waiting to be dirty; and Cheese's mother was always moving. Cleaning, wiping, cooking, shouting. But now it was all stopped, she wasn't doing anything. Cheese knew that grown-ups were funny like that. They just stopped in the middle of stuff all the time. It didn't matter what they were doing. Like the time Cheese had sneaked downstairs late to watch television and there was all this noise from his parents' bedroom overhead, like people walking around but it wasn't walking. It was too regular. And then it just stopped, suddenly stopped, no warning, and Cheese became aware of how loud the television was and he got up to turn it down; the remote control had had no batteries for ages. That was a good while ago though and Cheese knew what the noise meant now. They learnt all about sex at school years ago. The teacher's red face was the best part.

What's wrong Mam?

Cheese had broken the silence with an enquiry. He hoped his tone of voice was the right one. He looked up from Emma's fat little baby face to see his mother still standing there, with her chin on her chest, not moving except for the up-down sobbing shake of her hunched shoulders. Cheese's mother was taller than the other mothers. The sink was too low.

Nothing Eamon, nothing

and she didn't turn around but she started to move her hands again. Plate, wipe, rinse, plate, and somehow it was better; the kitchen was moving again, and the kitchen was always moving. Cheese felt a massive release, of tension I suppose, but to a twelve-year-old tension probably means fear. Everything was alright, but it wasn't, *not really*. Cheese knew you couldn't trust grown-ups. They were expert, *professional*, at saying something and not meaning it.

We'll be going now in a minute Eamon

This was Cheese's dad's standard response when he caught his son staring at him through the stinging cigarette smoke of his local. The premise to a broken promise. *No way are we going in a minute.* Cheese knew.

Okay dad

Good lad Eamon, good lad

And then a few minutes later, inevitably, a full drink would arrive in front of his father and another glass of Coke would be deposited in front of Cheese. Or orange. Or anything.

We'll be gone in just a minute Eamon, a short while now

And Cheese would sit and stare at the ashtray full of empty crisp packets that wouldn't stay folded and curse his father. One more drink meant two, everyone knew that. His father would have to buy one back for the guy he was drinking with. It was just like multiplication tables at school; if two men were drinking, they could never have an uneven number of drinks. Two multiplied by one is two. It was worse if there was three of them, because one more drink meant three more. *Three ones is three, three twos is six, three threes is nine.*

More Coke, are you alright for the crisps there Eamon?

Shut up, shut up, why won't you shut up? Cheese clamped his hands back on his ears. It was nearly one o'clock. It was always nearly one o' clock it happened. The evening wouldn't be too bad, it could be good sometimes, with his mother, some dinner, homework, television, Emma. He would throw her in the air watching her face go red and round with that huge baby grin while his hands waited that long second before they would catch her. His mother always shouted at him to stop, *you'll drop her Eamon, stop*, but Cheese knew he couldn't hurt her. Not Emma, no way. And then there was bedtime, and squeezing an extra half an hour out of his mother, *please Eamon, please just go to bed*, and

Eamon would finally go. He always went just before she got angry, and he didn't want to make her angry. It was nice like that, just the three of them, and the night-time and the television. Sometimes they might play cards, snap mostly. Cheese always won but his mother never seemed to mind, they would always share his prize, some chocolate usually, or maybe a small packet of Opal Fruits. Opal Fruits were his favourite. Sometimes they talked about Emma, and laughed about Emma. She was really stupid sometimes, you had to laugh because it hurt if you didn't. It was really nice. *One plus one plus one is three.* Cheese liked it when his mother laughed. He could see her gold tooth. Her head thrown back and her mouth wide open, and her hair everywhere.

A present from your father

his mother had said when she showed it to him the day she arrived back from the hospital. His grandmother had looked after him while his mother was away, *same old ding-dong Eamon, same old ding-dong.* Emma hadn't been around then. Cheese looked up through the darkness at the dull gleam of the metal rail overhead and the clothes he never wore, and remembered that night his mother came home was the first night he had sat there. He had been looking for something, he couldn't remember what exactly. That's when it started, the shouting.

Well I hope you're proud of yourself

And so it began. His father's response had been so loud and terrifying that Cheese jerked his foot forward and allowed the wardrobe door to close behind him. And he had sat there. Just sat there and waited for it to end. It was so dark, but Cheese liked that, he liked how his world could suddenly get so small. It was safe there and it was his. The box he sat on had gotten fuller since that first time of course, more old shoes and more old books that he had grown out of. And secrets, many more secrets. Hidden in its layers was the archaeology of the days and nights Cheese had lived since then; a valentine he had got from a girl at his school, a picture of a naked woman with dark hair between her legs,

go on Cheese take it yacanseefannyaneverytin

and three cigarettes he had seen on the ground on the way home from school a few months ago and for some reason had picked up. Christ, the anxiety that day. He had run straight upstairs, opened the wardrobe door and hid them right at the bottom of the box. The very bottom, beneath the books, shoes, the valentine, the broken lampshade, the tinily folded picture of the woman, his savings, everything. The cigarettes were still there now, Cheese didn't like smoking. The crushed picture of the naked girl was still there too, in the empty battery compartment of the broken radio he could feel sticking into his lower back. Cheese didn't want to throw it out, he didn't want his mother to find it in the rubbish. He didn't want her to think he owned it. One of Emma's soft toys was there as well, Ernie from Sesame Street. Emma was too young to remember Sesame Street, it hadn't been on for ages, but she liked Ernie's green trousers. She always pointed at anything green, or grabbed at anything green, like the curtains in the living room, she was always trying to pull them down, sitting on the floor and grabbing.

It was cold now and Cheese let his hands clutch his knees to his chest. It was quiet downstairs so he could leave them there. They didn't have to muffle the noise any more so he could use them to warm himself, because it was so cold tonight, so cold. Cheese reached overhead and felt in the darkness for some clothes, any clothes, something to wrap around himself to keep warm before he got back into bed. He grimaced as he remembered that the bed would long ago have lost its body warmth heat. Cheese would have to do it all over again.

That night, and the wind-chime quivering of the clothes hangers; that is what Cheese remembered as he looked down at the prostrate blonde sprawled on his bedroom floor. The bruise on the side of her face was rising rapidly, but Cheese wasn't sorry, no way. He was sick of people calling him by his nickname and he had warned her, warned her more than once, the minute he had been introduced as Cheese he had corrected the lads, *Eamon*, he had told her, *Eamon*. Cheese didn't know why this is what he remembered now, he hadn't thought about it for years. Decades. He lit a cigarette anyway, and lifted her skirt with his free hand. Her *tarty black skirt. Fuckin' tart.* And then it was forgotten, completely. The wardrobe, the shoes, the cold, everything. Cheese pulled her underwear down over her legs and with the back of his hand felt her dry and coarse. He put his cigarette in the ashtray, spat on his palm and rubbed her dryness, rubbed the sandpapery fuzz between her legs and the treasure it hid.

my name is Eamon, Cheese muttered beneath his own beer haze, *my name is Eamon*.

Short list

These are the writers who made the short list in the 1999 prize.

Marie Altzinger
Kristina Una Amadeus
Celeste Auge
Shauna Singh Baldwin
Kevin Brooks
Tom Bryan
Elizabeth Carthy
June Coyle
Catherine Czerkawska
Gill Davis
Eileen Donovan-Kranz
Peter Dorward
Stella Pope Duarte
Helen Fallon
Amanda Fergusson
Janice Fox
Richard Goodson
John Grove-Stephenson
Sian Hughes
William Kanouse
Linda Kantner
Carla Lamont

John Latham
David Lewis
Justin Lynham
Marie MacSweeney
Carmel Maginn
Adrianne Marcus
Paul Michel
Patricia Middleton
Paul Milican
Dana Murphy
Cormac O'Leary
Kevin Parry
Janak Raj
Dorothy Reinders
Valerie Sirr
Rebecca Smith
Stuart Tallack
Nicola Taylor
William Wall
Allan Wells
Sue Wood
Howard Wright

Prizes

First Prize :
£1,000 (approx $1,500)

Second Prizes (to be awarded to the two second-best stories) :
- One week at Anam Cara Writers' and Artists' Retreat.
  Contact: Sue Booth-Forbes.

Address: Eyeries, The Beara Peninsula, Co. Cork, Ireland.
Tel: 00 353 (0)27 74441
E Mail: anamcararetreat@tinet.ie
Website: www.ugr.com/anamcararetreat/
Situated in one of the most rugged and beautiful parts of Ireland
overlooking Kenmare Bay, this is an ideal place to write. Also to walk,
swim, fish, read, or take a drink in the pubs of the idyllic town of
Eyeries. It is run by Sue Booth-Forbes, who lends a personal touch to
this unique set-up.

- A weekend residential writing course from the Dingle Writing
  Courses 2000 Programme.

Contact: Nicholas McLachlan or Abigail Joffe.
Address: Dingle Writing Courses Ltd Ballintlea, Ventry, Co. Kerry,
Ireland.
Tel: 00 353 (0)66 91 59052
E mail: dinglewc@iol.ie
Website: www.iol.ie/~dinglewc
On the stunning Dingle Peninsula in Co. Kerry, overlooking the
magnificent Inch Beach, a few miles from the town of Dingle, the
courses here are much sought after. Tutors have included novelists
Jennifer Johnston, Anne Enright, theatre director David Byrne,
playwright Vincent Woods, and poets Pat Boran, Paul Durcan, and
Graham Mort.

Fish Publishing Annual Short Story Prize.

£1,000 for the overall winner.
Second Prizes:
week at writers' retreat,
weekend writing course
Top 15 stories will be published in Fish's next anthology.

Judges:
William Wharton, Julia Darling, Dermot Bolger.

Conditions:
- Stories must not exceed 5,000 words. There is no minimum.
- They must be typed, one side, 1.5 spacing (min).
- Name and address should not appear on text, but on a separate sheet.
- A fee of £8 for the first story is required, £5.00 per subsequent story. £5.00 per story for full-time students, pensioners and the unemployed.
- The judges' verdict is final. No correspondence will be entered into once work has been submitted.
- If receipt of entry, notification of results, or any other information is needed it is necessary to include a SAE. Stories will not be returned.
- **Closing date 30th Nov., every year.**
- Results announced 17th March on our website.
- The winning stories must be available to *Fish* for the forthcoming anthology, and therefore must not have been published previously.
- Entry will be deemed as acceptance of these conditions.
- No entry form is needed.

Send stories to:-

Fish Short Story Prize
Durrus, Bantry, Co. Cork, Ireland.
E mail: fishpublishing@tinet.ie

Honorary Patrons: *Roddy Doyle, Dermot Healy.*
(Conditions may alter slightly in future years, see our web site for updates –
www.sleeping-giant.ie/fishpublishing)